AN APOLOGETICS STUDY FOR STUDENTS

TRUTH *Matters*

CONFIDENT FAITH
IN A CONFUSING WORLD

ANDREAS KÖSTENBERGER,
DARRELL BOCK, & JOSH CHATRAW

ISBN: 978-1-4300-3251-9
Item Number: 005647989

Dewey Decimal Classification Number: 177
Subject Heading: TRUTH \ HONESTY \ VALUES

Printed in the United States of America

We believe that the Bible has God for its author; salvation for its end; and truth, without any mixture of error, for its matter and that all Scripture is totally true and trustworthy. To review LifeWay's doctrinal guideline, please visit *www.lifeway.com/doctrinalguideline.*

Student Ministry Publishing
LifeWay Church Resources
One LifeWay Plaza
Nashville, TN 37234-0144

TABLE OF CONTENTS

HOW TO USE

This resource is an apologetics study based on the trade book, *Truth Matters*. While all of the material in the Leader Guide is sufficent to be able to lead a group of students through the study, we encourage you to also consult the corresponding chapters in the trade book for additional content to help you prepare.

You can use this resource as a short-term weekly study, or in a weekend retreat. However, we encourage you to provide adequate time for group discussion. The nature of the study will lend itself to questions that will take time to answer and discuss.

SECTIONS OF THE STUDY

» OPENING

This section provides an activity to introduce the topic and get the discussion started.

» THE STORY

Following the Opening will be a story or scenario to illustrate the session's topic. The students will be asked how to respond based on what they know and believe at this point. The students can read this silently or you or a student could read it aloud.

» THE QUESTION

Each session will focus on one question that students may face in defending their faith. Allow students to make an initial response to the question.

» THE SKEPTIC'S VIEW

This section will briefly describe how a skeptic of Christianity would or does answer the Question. Their view is not totally captured here, but will be further fleshed out throughout the session.

» THE RESPONSE

This is the largest section in the session, providing information to help students answer the skeptic. Several points will be presented along with questions and information to help equip your students to be able to defend their faith.

» GROUP DISCUSSION

Several questions will be provided to help you gauge the students' understanding of the session material. Feel free to provide additional questions as you see fit based upon the nature of your group.

» CLOSING THOUGHTS

This information will help you summarize the session and reinforce the main points you have discussed.

» APPLICATION

Two kinds of application need to take place with an apologetics study: personal and missional.

- » **PERSONAL:** Each session should help students strengthen their own faith by providing additional support for what they believe.

- » **MISSIONAL:** Each session should also help students know and be able to articulate what they believe and why, not so they can win arguments, but so they can better share the gospel and "give a reason for the hope that is within them."

Don't rush through this section. Provide time for each student to evaluate, and some students to articulate, the application they take from the study.

» CONTINUE THE STORY

To close the session, return to The Story and allow students to respond again to the scenario, now based on what they have learned in the session.

TEACHING ELEMENTS

» ASK

Most of the session is discussion-based, therefore you will be prompted to ask questions throughout. Additional questions are provided in the leader guide that are not present in the student book.

» STATE AND DISCUSS

Key statements from the *Truth Matters* book and other sources will be highlighted for discussion.

Teaching material is provided to help you lead your sessions.
The sections highlighted by the black bar indicates information also found in the student book.

Other teaching help is provided when you see the following symbol:
Again, we encourage you to refer to the trade book for added help.

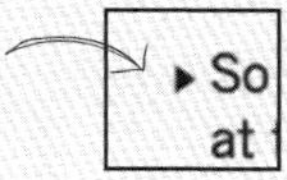

SESSION 1

A REASONABLE FAITH

OPENING

Write several false or nonsense statements on index cards, one statement per card. Place all the cards in a paper bag. (Examples: The sun is actually powered by your local electric company. / Playing sports is actually bad for your body. / Ketchup and mustard are made from the same ingredients, etc.) Call on volunteers to come to the front of the room, one at a time, and draw one statement from the bag. Instruct the student that he/she is to defend the validity of the statement. Give the volunteer 30 seconds to consider how to defend, then instruct him/her to read the statement aloud. Students should ask questions that attack the statement and the volunteer must defend the statement. Allow several students to defend statements.

» **ASK:** What was hard about defending your statement? Have you ever felt that way when trying to defend what you believe? Explain.

THE STORY

There I was, sitting in church with my head down and my eyes closed, asking Jesus to come into my heart—once again. Don't worry, I wasn't alone—pretty much the entire congregation was doing it with me at the time. The reason being is because we had an evangelist come to our church that evening who said, quite emphatically, "If you are 99% sure you're saved, and 1% doubting, then you are a 100% lost!"

Who could argue with that mathematical argument? I knew my own heart, and knew that I had been dealing with doubts or questions—intellectual roadblocks if you will. I wanted to overcome these, and according to him, the way I could do that was to say the sinner's prayer once more.

Come to find out, the evangelist, even though he meant well, was wrong in what he said. Being a genuine follower of Christ, one who has been transformed from the inside out, doesn't mean one will never experience doubt or have questions that arise. Doubts don't equal unbelief, in the same way that a lack of knowledge over how my car works doesn't lead me to abandon it altogether. Unlike unbelief, doubts are simply mental roadblocks that need to be overcome and answered by the person having them.

I was already a Christian at that time, and like other young believers who are growing in their knowledge of God, I had questions that would often come up. My questions and doubts had nothing to do with the truthfulness of the Christian worldview – quite the opposite, they had to do with my lack of understanding. It was like being in biology class for only a week – I was able to pick up a lot of foundational things, but still had much more to learn. Thankfully, I had people and influences in my life that helped me think through the things I was wrestling with mentally. And it was during this time that I heard about Christian apologetics (which simply means a reasoned defense of the Christian faith). Apologetics not only helped me to see that I wasn't the only one with similar questions, but also gave me the resources and tools to think deeply about the things I believe. Something you are about to do throughout this study.

THE QUESTION

Call on a student to read the question for the session:

Isn't Christianity all about faith and not reason?

FIRST RESPONSE

» **ASK:** If you had to answer that question today, how would you respond?

» THE SKEPTIC'S VIEW

Discuss the skeptic's view of this issue using the information below.

It's probably no surprise to you that there are those who question the validity of the Christian faith. The doctrines and beliefs that we, as followers of Christ, hold dear and base our faith on, they scoff at and try desperately to punch holes in. In this study, we will refer to these people as skeptics.

What is a skeptic?

A skeptic is a person who has an attitude of judgment against, and frequently criticizes, religious beliefs.

What does a skeptic look like?

These days, a skeptic could take on the form of your Biology teacher, a Hollywood celebrity, the new kid in class, your college professor, a TV talkshow host, even one of your friends at church. Religious skepticism abounds, and seems to be growing in our world of tolerance and acceptance.

Why is their voice heard and their arguments given such credence?

1) **Their arguments sound good.** Some skeptics can state their case in eloquent and convincing fashion. They will even use compelling, personal stories of their own journey of questions and doubts that led them to abandon the faith. But truth is not confirmed or denied based on heart-stirring stories.

» **ASK:** Have you ever heard a skeptic give a stirring argument for his or her belief? Were they convincing? Explain.

2) **We are vulnerable.** Most of us have not invested much time in studying the foundations of our faith. We don't know much, if anything ,about the origins of Scripture. We haven't contemplated the reason for suffering and evil, or how we would prove the historicity of the resurrection. We know what our personal experience with God has been like, but not much beyond that. So, when the skeptic asks hard questions and speaks with authority on issues, we don't know how to respond.

» **ASK:** So, have you ever thought much about the deep or hard questions about origin of Scripture, the problem of suffering and evil, and proof of the resurrection? Why or why not?

3) **We live in a world where tolerance is king.** To hold to the exclusive truth claims of Christianity, such as Jesus being the only way of salvation, puts us in an ever-increasing minority. While our beliefs are seen as backward, out-of-date, and intolerant, the skeptic's views are welcomed and seen as more enlightened.

» **ASK:** Do you agree with this statement? Have you ever faced opposition because you held to our exclusive truth claims? Explain.

4) **They pit** faith **vs.** reason. The skeptic wants to say that if you choose Christian faith, you check your brain at the door. And in the past, believers haven't done much to combat that. We've made faith about what we feel, about our heart and emotions. However, faith and intellect should go together.

» **ASK:** Do you think faith and intellect can really go together? Explain.

THE RESPONSE

» WHY STUDY APOLOGETICS?

Discuss the following material to reinforce the reason an apologetics study is so important.

1) Apologetics helps us to better understand our faith. Not only that, but apologetics also helps to increase our faith commitment. As Christians we are charged with the task of not only knowing "what" we believe, but also "why" we believe it.

» **STATE AND DISCUSS:** "Few issues plague believers more frequently than doubts concerning Christianity in general or their own faith in particular."

- That means we are not to simply inherit a faith from our family or borrow the faith of our friends – instead we are to be the vibrant owners of the Christian faith ourselves. And knowing the reasons for our beliefs will help us reach that goal.

Call on a student to read 1 Corinthians 14:20.

Brothers, don't be childish in your thinking, but be infants in regard to evil and adult in your thinking.

1 CORINTHIANS 14:20

» **ASK:** Based off this verse, what is the difference between a childlike faith and a childish faith? Which one should Christians pursue? Which one are you currently pursuing?

Point out that a childlike faith is a growing, maturing faith.

2) Apologetics shows us that faith is not at odds with reason. Many of the critics we will see throughout this study misunderstand what the Christian worldview means by faith.

- In fact, most people in our culture choose to pocket away the concept of faith as a mere personal preference, neither expecting nor requiring it to be grounded in reason, logic, and historical realities. Faith is just something you accept. It doesn't need to be burdened with making rational sense. It just . . . Is.

Faith, however, does not need to be blind. Believing in Christ and accepting the Bible as his true Word is not automatic anti-intellectualism. The Bible doesn't ask us to adopt a BLIND faith but a REASONED faith—a faith that can honestly ask the hard questions and then go out in search of real, measurable, credible answers.

- Paul was definitely a proponent of reasoned faith. When he made his case to the Corinthians for the reliability of Jesus' resurrection, he didn't tell them to accept this key doctrine of the church just because he said so. He first referred to written documentation:

Call on a student to read 1 Corinthians 15:3-4.

That Christ died for our sins according to the Scriptures, that He was buried, that He was raised on the third day according to the Scriptures.
1 CORINTHIANS 15:3–4

» **ASK:** Is Paul advocating for a blind faith or a reasoned faith? Explain. Could you describe your faith as a reasoned faith? Why or why not? Which can stand up to the skeptics? Explain.

Use the following information to help reinforce Paul's emphasis on a reasoned faith.

Paul backed up his claim with eyewitness testimony, saying that Jesus "appeared to Cephas, then to the Twelve. Then He appeared to over 500 brothers at one time; most of them are still alive" (vv. 5–6).

Paul conceded that if his assertions about the resurrection of Christ didn't hold water, "then our proclamation is without foundation, and so is your faith" (v. 14). In other words, if you can give me no proof whatsoever that Jesus did what He said He did, then you really have no reason to believe in Him. That's why Paul's comment that "most" of the eyewitnesses to Jesus' life, death, and resurrection were "still alive" is so impressive. It's one thing for him to say the risen Christ was seen by a bunch of people who could never be confronted or challenged to their face, whose story could never be interviewed for inconsistencies. It's quite another to dare someone to go find somebody who was actually there: Ask them whatever you want! See if they don't tell you the same thing! Paul wasn't afraid of people following up the evidence. In fact, he encouraged this kind of historical investigation.

3) Apologetics helps give us a reasoned <u>defense</u> against <u>critics</u>. Faith is reasonable—whether critics want you to know it or not.

- Authors, speakers, and professors who are hostile towards Christianity are banking on the assumption that if you find their appeals to reason stimulating, you won't feel like you can bring your faith along when you go exploring out there.

They want you to believe that faith can only play within safe, churchy cloisters where it doesn't need to validate itself against anything other than itself. However, as you'll see throughout, the problem is not that they're making historical accusations against orthodox Christian faith. That's fine. Our problem is that their arguments are simply not the best ones, the most likely ones, the most reasonable ones.

» **STATE AND DISCUSS:** A dog barks when his master is attacked. I would be a coward if I saw that God's truth is attacked and yet would remain silent." –John Calvin

» WARNING!

Discuss the following information, noting the emphasis on not allowing our faith to just be an intellectual exercise.

So have fun, learn, and allow this study to stretch and grow you in your walk with Christ. Walk in the comfort and confidence of a reasoned faith beyond the challenge of the skeptic. Yet while doing so, be careful to not sink so deeply into the mission of defending your faith as to reduce belief to intellectual acceptance. The sky is blue, the grass is green, and Jesus rose from the dead, stated as if they're each of equal importance and consequence. No, your faith in Christ is not only well placed because it makes reasonable sense, against all other worldviews and patterns of thought, but because this Jesus can change you and us and inspire us to lives that brim with our created purpose.

» **ASK:** What is the danger of reducing our beliefs to intellectual acceptance?

- Reasoned faith is all-purpose faith. It is the type of faith that moves from the head to the heart and from the heart to the hands. It is the type of faith that allows God's truth to course through the head and the heart, changing the person from the inside out. And once this takes place, it gives rise to outward ways of living in all aspects of life, whether from behind a school desk or across the table from friends.

» **ASK:** How does a reasoned faith influence every part of one's life? What are some examples?

Stay in the Scripture, not merely to prove it true but to show that it's alive and enlightening, transforming you into someone who thinks, acts, speaks, and responds with Christlike character because of the Holy Spirit that works inside you. The God whose eternal truth and nature stand behind the Bible is not only your champion as you claim that truth matters, but is also for your heart and soul as a devoted believer. Be His disciple as well as His defender, and you will love the places your reasoned faith in Him can take you.

Call on a student to read John 8:32.

You will know the truth, and the truth will set you free.
JOHN 8:32

» **ASK:** Why do you think it is important to focus on truth? How can knowing the truth be freeing? What does this look like on a daily basis? Are you focused on the truth? Why or why not?

GROUP DISCUSSION

» 1) What are some doubts or critiques you've heard about the Bible and Christianity? What are some of your own doubts?

» 2) What is the difference between blind and reasoned faith?

» 3) How would you go about pursuing a reasoned faith?

» 4) Do you consider yourself prepared to give a defense of the Christian worldview if asked? How can you make sure you stay in the Scriptures so that when questions come you know what the Bible teaches on a given subject?

CLOSING THOUGHTS

Use the following information to summarize and reinforce key points in the session.

C.S. Lewis once said, "I believe in Christianity as I believe the sun has risen. Not only because I see it, but because by it I see everything else." This quote affirms the fact that the Christian worldview makes sense—it is reasonable, coherent, and compelling—but also the fact that it helps makes sense of all other aspects of life.

The task of apologetics is to help connect those dots so that both believers and non-believers are able to see that. If you are a believer, apologetics will help strengthen your own faith and help you overcome any mental roadblocks you are having.

But in addition to increasing our own faith, apologetics is to be used as a witnessing tool as we live on mission for Jesus. Christians are a missional group of people. Just as our God set out on mission to rescue and redeem us, we too are to live our lives with the intention of sharing and displaying the gospel to those around us.

By focusing on these truths, we accomplish at least two things:

» 1) We move forward in our maturity as believers in Christ.

» 2) We grow stronger in the defense of our beliefs as we begin to understand "why" it is we believe what we do.

APPLICATION

Remind students that as we saw in this session, it is important to never separate the mind from the heart and hands. In light of that, direct students to spend some time reflecting/writing on how this session challenges them both inwardly and outwardly.

PERSONAL:

1) How has the information in this session strengthened your personal faith in God?

MISSIONAL:

2) How has the information in this session helped prepare you to answer the skeptics and share with the unsaved?

CONTINUE THE STORY

Direct students to write their own personal story of coming to faith in Christ, and whether their Christian walk up to this point has included any doubts or questions. Encourage them to list the questions and doubts and how they have approached them.

Take a few minutes to discuss the students' responses, reminding them of the difference in disbelief and doubt. Relate to students that you are available to pray with them and further discuss these matters to help them work through lingering issues.

SESSION 2

IS GOD THERE? DOES GOD CARE?

OPENING

Perform an illusion or card trick, or enlist a student or another adult to do so. If no one is able to do this, show a video of an illusion or card trick from the Internet. After the trick has been performed, ask students to explain what happened.

» **ASK:** Would you say that every illusion or trick has an explanation? Why? Would you say that most things that happen in life have an explanation? Are there some things that happen that we struggle to explain? Why?

Point out that while every card trick or magician's illusion has an explanation, not every life event can make that claim. There are things that happen that we don't understand, especially when it comes to suffering and evil. The skeptic wants to use that to defame God's character and challenge His existence.

THE STORY

For the most part it was a typical Wednesday night at the student group. I brought some snacks, and there was the weekly guys versus girls foosball competition leading up to our group time. On the surface, everything appeared to be normal, but it was not. While the group went through the usual routine, it was clear they were merely moving through the motions. Something else was on their mind.

Everyone was there – that is, with the exception of Tony. In fact, Tony's absence was the reason behind the mood that evening. Tony, a beloved 16-year-old member of our group, was nearing the end of his battle with terminal cancer.

That evening we continued our study on the nature of God, giving special attention to His all-powerful rule and control over the universe. I wasn't surprised when one of the students, Amy, blurted out during teaching time, "If God is so powerful and so loving, why doesn't He heal Tony and prevent him from dying?" She wasn't the only one thinking it.

THE QUESTION

Call on a student to read the question for the session:

If there really is a God, then why is there so much suffering and evil in the world?

» **ASK:** If you had to answer that question today, how would you respond?

THE SKEPTIC'S VIEW

Discuss the skeptic's view of this issue using the information below. Make sure students understand the phrase "arguments from evil."

Amy wasn't the first to ever wonder why evil exists in a world that is ruled by a good and sovereign God. In fact, as we will see, this is probably one of the most often voiced objections against the Christian faith. Objections like these are what have come to be known as the "arguments from evil."

The basic pattern of these arguments is pretty simple to follow. Skeptics will say that the existence of an all-powerful, all-loving God doesn't seem to square with the existence of evil in the world. Since there is evil of all sorts, then according to them it must mean that God is not powerful enough to stop it, or can, but is indifferent to our suffering, or both. For them, either of these outcomes points to the belief that God does not exist.

But what if God has good reasons—reasons that we can know, and perhaps some that we can't—for allowing evil to exist? Because of this simple fact, atheists hardly ever use the argument in this fashion anymore. It simply fails. However, they still use the arguments from evil as a way to get an emotional response. If they can hook you emotionally, perhaps you'll continue along for the ride.

» BEHIND THE WORDS:

» **ASK:** Do you understand their reasoning? Explain.

» **ASK:** What is a first step in being able to defend your faith against the skeptic's reasoning?

- First step in answering this objection is to pay attention to what is truly being said.
- Follow their statements closely, like following the various wires and cables that snake behind your television—you find the one that actually plugs into the wall.
- Once you pay closer attention, you can ask: What's at the bottom of his statement? What are they really saying when they call God out for what he's doing, when they challenge what they perceive to be the way God operates?

In this instance, here is what they are saying:

"God, you cannot be good."
"You shouldn't do it like this."
"You should know better."
"If you're real (and that's a big IF), you are seriously not handling things right."

» **ASK:** Does this make sense? What is the flaw with this type of thinking?

» **ASK:** Do you know someone who is struggling like this? Have you ever struggled with these kinds of thoughts? Explain.

» THE RESPONSE

1) GOT TO HAVE A STANDARD

» **ASK:** While your car is in the school parking lot, a random student shows up and washes your windshield. Five minutes later, another student takes a baseball bat and smashes your windshield. Which of these students did the wrong thing? Based on what?

Discuss the following information, emphasizing that if there is no absolute standard, then what's right and what's wrong are subject to whoever makes the rules.

If someone says that what God is doing is wrong, how do we know that? How can we judge His actions to be cruel and immoral? What standard do we use to measure the rightness or wrongness of His behavior? Or of anyone's behavior? If there's no God, if there's no Word, no truth, no ultimate standard of right and wrong, then what makes someone who busts out your windshield any more wrong than if they wash your car or buy you a tank of gas? Without something or someone, somewhere in the universe, to frame our existence in such a way that certain actions are good and others are evil, on what grounds do we decide which is which?

» **STATE AND DISCUSS:** "Apart from an ultimate standard and source for morality, there cannot be wrong actions."

» **ASK:** On what do we base our standard of right and wrong?

» **ASK:** Why does most of the world have a problem with our standard?

Point out that, as followers of Christ, we believe our standard for what is right comes from the character of God, knowing that He is the source of all goodness. However, the atheistic worldview cannot accept that. Use the following information to explain:

For them, if there is no mind or Creator behind our existence, then we're just a conglomeration of atoms. There is no god, good or bad. So they're asking us to believe that these skin cells and blood vessels and brain matter and bone fragments somehow got together—along with all the other material components of our world—and hashed out a code of morality for ourselves. But if we are no more than evolutionary beings with no Creator to whom we are accountable, then this play-nice morality goes against our essence as individuals. There is simply no rational space within this worldview for people being nice to one another. However, if you allow for real goodness and evil in the world, then we would have to allow for the existence of God given that He is the only standard that divides what is good between what is evil.

- The Bible tells us that from birth we were given a conscience, something within us that instinctively points us to what is right and good.
- The Scripture also states that we were created in His image, created for relationship with Him and with others. And that our capacity for good reflects His capacity for good.

Walk students through the diagram on page 16 in the student book to help them understand:

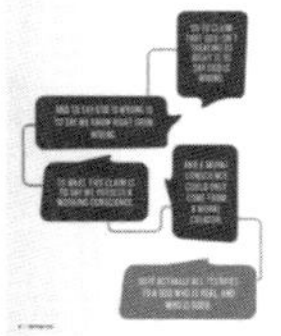

- So to claim that God isn't treating us right is to say God is wrong.
- And to say God is wrong is to say we know right from wrong.
- To make this claim is to say we possess a working conscience.
- And a moral conscience could only come from a moral Creator.
- So it actually all testifies to a God who is real. And who is good.

2) THE QUESTION OF SUFFERING

» ASK: Why does suffering in our world call God's character and existence into question? Has this question of suffering ever affected your faith in God? Explain.

Discuss:

Most of people's doubts about God in relation to suffering stem from two taproots:

1) a refusal to see God as having divine rights over His creation

2) a minimization of the extent of human rebellion against our Creator

#1 DIVINE RIGHTS

» ASK: When we say God has divine rights over His creation, what do we mean?

» STATE AND DISCUSS: "If God is God, as the Bible clearly asserts, then He doesn't need anyone's permission to do anything He wants."

» ASK: How do you respond to that statement?

Use the following information to help students understand that just because we don't like or understand an aspect of God's character doesn't mean it's not true.

We may not like that. But if someone wants to challenge the biblical truth that God is God and is therefore entitled to banish a soul to hell, for example, we need to hear them doing more than just standing over there and expressing their personal disdain for it. Show us, from what the Bible teaches, why God's actions must meet with your and our approval.

Share and discuss the following story from Tim Keller to explain this point:

Tim Keller writes of a discussion he had with a woman who shared this type of outrage at God's entitled role as judge. He asked if she was equally offended by the idea of God being forgiving and merciful. Of course not. And yet in some corners of the world, that's exactly how people feel. Secular Westerners like us, Keller explained, almost inherently recoil at the Christian doctrine of hell, and yet we generally find the Bible's teachings on forgiveness and turning the other cheek to be quite appealing. Traditional societies, however, tend to have a lot less problem accepting the idea of God's judgment than they do the biblical notion of mercy. The whole idea of releasing a debt seems abhorrent to them—the same kind of reaction we may feel when we hear about lakes of fire and eternal gnashing of teeth. They are "offended" by a forgiving God, just as we are conditioned to take more natural offense at his judgment and his justice. Keller concluded by saying to the woman, "Why should cultural sensibilities be the final court in which to judge whether Christianity is valid?"[1]

> **≫ ASK:** Do you agree or disagree with Tim Keller? Explain.

Discuss the following, emphasizing that if God really is God, He can do as He pleases.

Have you ever thought of it that way? What gives twenty-first century American poll results the final call on what's acceptable about God's nature and character? How dare they not check with us first? But if God is God—that's the biblical position—what makes Him wrong to choose His own actions?

#2 THE FALL

> **≫ ASK:** What do we mean by the fall? Why is understanding the effect of the fall so crucial to understanding the reality of suffering?

- If someone underestimates the effects of this one reality on human existence, he or she will never succeed at delving fully into these "problem" areas with the Bible.

Discuss the following with students. Help them understand that if we neglect the effects of the fall, then we will never get a grip on the tough teachings in Scripture:

In a general sense, all suffering is rooted in rebellion against God. There was no suffering of any kind in the garden of Eden in which he placed the first man and woman. But when they sinned, the perfection of God's created order twisted into a downward spiral. And each successive generation, each person who's ever lived—us!—we're all part of the rebellion. We don't deserve free and easy lives.

> **≫ ASK:** Are you a sinner? Think back over the last 24 hours and mentally list all the sins you've committed.

Discuss the following, emphasizing that all of us are sinners, and regardless of the nature of our sinful actions, all sin is rebellion against God.

- Most people see evil just on the horizontal level—people harming other people.
- The Bible, however, affirms that even the man-on-man, relational nature of evil and suffering is in essence a vertical rebellion against God, His authority, His principles, and His rule.
- Example of this truth: King David, after committing adultery and murder, confessed to God, "Against You—You alone—I have sinned and done this evil in Your sight" (Ps. 51:4)
- And all of us are guilty. Romans 3:23 confirms we were all born with a nature that rebels against God.

Obeying Him is tough on us. Sinning, by contrast, is a piece of cake. We are hard-wired to ignore Him, to overrule Him, to do whatever we want. And we do it without even stopping to realize that the effort required to sin against Him is only ours because He gave it to us.

So when seen from this most basic of biblical views—the doctrine of sin and the fall—the real mystery is not that we suffer. The mystery is that He's ever let us enjoy any blessing at all: the simple pleasure of a smile, a laugh, a walk in the grass, the strength for an afternoon workout, the warmth of family and friends. Perhaps from this perspective we might actually ponder the "problem of good"—why any of us should experience the abundant, though often unnoticed, presence of mercy and provision in our daily lives.

3) JESUS AND THE PROBLEM OF SUFFERING

When it comes to understanding our own personal suffering and pain, it is crucial to remember this essential truth to the Christian worldview: God's incarnation in Christ.

>> **STATE AND DISCUSS:** "When God sent His Son to suffer, He made the boldest statement of all about suffering."

Lead students to find these Scripture passages and record some of the sufferings of Jesus.

Matthew 4:1-11

Luke 22:39-47

Mark 14:60-72

John 19:1-18

>> **ASK:** Can you think of other ways Jesus suffered while on earth?

Use the information below to discuss the sufferings of Christ:

Even if Christ's coming doesn't answer every one of our specific questions, the Bible does say that Jesus entered our world and suffered alongside His people, "becoming obedient to the point of death—even to death on a cross" (Phil. 2:8). "For we do not have a high priest who is unable to sympathize with our weaknesses, but One who has been tested in every way as we are" (Heb. 4:15)—"despised and rejected by men, a man of suffering" (Isa. 53:3).

- God may not always explain why things happen, but through Christ, He has shown His love for us.
- He also has shown time and again that He can provide joy even in the midst of our greatest suffering.

» **ASK:** How does the suffering of Jesus help answer those who would question God's character and actions?

Call on a volunteer to read aloud the Alvin Plantinga quote below, then discuss.

"It would be easy to see God as remote and detached, permitting all these evils, Himself untouched, in order to achieve ends that are no doubt exalted but have little to do with us, and little power to assuage our griefs. It would be easy to see Him as cold and unfeeling—or if loving, then such that His love for us has little to do with our perception of our own welfare. But God, as Christians see Him, is neither remote nor detached. His aims and goals may be beyond our ken and may require our suffering, but He is Himself prepared to accept much greater suffering in the pursuit of those ends."[2]

GROUP DISCUSSION

» 1) How does the skeptic want to use the existence of suffering and evil as an argument against God's existence and character? Have you ever entertained that argument because of your own painful experiences?

» 2) How does a Christian understanding of Jesus' crucifixion help us deal with suffering?

» 3) If we were to imagine there was no God, what would that imply about suffering and evil?

» 4) Why can the existence of evil and suffering not disprove God, and how does it actually serve as a powerful argument for the existence of God?

CLOSING THOUGHTS

Discuss the closing thoughts to summarize and reinforce the main points of this session.

The critic's argument from evil is one that is unlike any other. For starters, its subject matter hits home for most of us, and in this sense, can be quite personal. Because of these harsh realities of pain and suffering, the critic has your attention and can capitalize on your situation by feeding you the line that if God exists, these things wouldn't have happened.

However, we have seen that such an argument is easier said than supported. In fact, we have seen quite the opposite—if God goes, then so does the good (and the bad also). If God does not exist, then there is nothing but pitiless indifference in a world that could care less about our struggles.

Of course, this picture of reality goes against everything we know intuitively. We know that good exists, that evil exists, and that this world is not the way things ought to be. We know that God is for us, and that despite our rebellion and inviting the consequences of our sin into our daily lives, He is at work, even now, to restore all things until they are made new. And

He does all of this not as some distant deity, but as one who has left His heavenly throne to become one of us so that we might have a High Priest who can identify with our sufferings, having expereinced tremendous suffering Himself.

By focusing on these truths, we accomplish at least two things:

» 1) We deepen our faith and trust in the One who has conquered sin and pain and evil and is ever working for our good and joy, and

» 2) We provide for the critic a reasonable defense of our beliefs, as well as a counter-argument against the objections they raise.

When it comes down to it, the arguments from evil carry no weight for the one willing to think through the personal pain to the reasons behind them.

APPLICATION

Remind students of the "head to heart to hand" model found in Session 1, then direct them to spend time reflecting/writing on how this session challenges them both inwardly and outwardly.

PERSONAL:

1) How has the information in this session strengthened your personal faith in God?

MISSIONAL:

2) How has the information in this session help prepare you to answer the skeptics and share with the unsaved?

CONTINUE THE STORY

Direct students to review the story found at the beginning of this session. Ask them how they would respond to Amy based upon what they have learned throughout this session?

Be sensitive to students who may have just experienced a similar situation of suffering or may be currently walking through one. If you have a student like this, circle your group around them and pray for them as you close.

SESSION 3

LET'S MAKE A BIBLE

OPENING

Group students into small teams and relate this fictional scenario and assignment:
We have been notified that we will no longer be able to use our whole Bible. We can only keep five of the 66 books. However we can choose which five to keep. Each team must decide which five books of the Bible they want to keep and why.

Give students 5-7 minutes to work, then let each group report.

> **ASK:** How difficult was it to choose which books to keep? What made it difficult? How did your team come to the decision on which books to keep? Do you think the Bible we use was constructed in this fashion? Why or why not?

THE STORY

It was my first week of class as a college freshman. Everything that week seemed incredible–new environment, new goals, new responsibilities, and new friends. Classes even seemed to be going well.

Toward the end of the first week we began discussing ancient literary genres and techniques in a literature course I was taking. I found it interesting because much of what we discussed had to do with the literature of the Bible. Being a Christian, I liked that.

I walked out of class that day with a guy, Dan, who I had met earlier that week. I asked him about the lecture, hoping for an opportunity to share the gospel. After asking about the lecture, Dan anxiously told me that while it may be okay to look at the Bible for literary development, he was not comfortable with looking at it from the viewpoint of it being historical. According to Dan, "the Bible is the simple, made-up product from a few people who were in authority back then."

THE QUESTION

Call on a student to read the question for the session:

How did we actually get the different books of the Bible?

FIRST RESPONSE

» **ASK:** If you had to answer that question today, how would you respond?

THE SKEPTIC'S VIEW

Discuss the skeptic's view of this issue using the information below.

For many skeptics, challenging the authenticity of the Bible is a main priority. Given that their arguments from evil have been known to fail, they think that their next best line of attack resides in attacking what Christians believe to be revealed and inspired by God—His Word.

One of their strategic ways in attacking the Bible consists in giving the impression that today's catalog of New Testament books were not the only ones back then. They would have us to believe that other "gospels" written by folks like Thomas or Mary were also being circulated during this time, and could just as easily have been selected to be in the Bible. The only reason those books weren't, they add, is because those in power ended up hammering out the books we know today in formal church councils during the fourth century A.D. Thus, for skeptics, the development of the New Testament canon (meaning a group of texts that are recognized as authoritative) was nothing more than a rubber-stamping of books by those in power of the institution.

But let's give a heads up from the start—the arguments against the origin of the New Testament are flimsy at best. The skeptics work really hard to question the origins and validity of this collection of writings, but the holes in their claims are large and mostly puzzling. That's because defending the composition of the New Testament is a position of total strength, bolstered by all kinds of reasonable evidence. And by the time you've plowed through these upcoming sessions, we think you'll see exactly what we're talking about.

THE RESPONSE

1) WHAT HISTORY REVEALS

Use the following information to help students understand how the body of Scripture we call the New Testament was formed.

The argument presented by Dan could not be further from the truth. In fact, by the time of the massive church meetings in the A.D. 300s, the canon of the New Testament had already been forming on its own—and had actually been closed to all newcomers—for generations.

» **ASK:** What do we mean by "canon of the New Testament"?

Discuss the following definition to help students understand the meaning of canon.
Canon: A group of texts that are recognized as authoritative.

Here is what we know. Evidence suggests the early church, whose structure began developing quickly after the ascension of Jesus and the startling events of Pentecost (Acts 2), became immediately aware they were dealing with something huge in regard to certain writings. Those texts quickly became useful and began to circulate between local churches. Raised on the canon of Jewish Scripture, they began to recognize that this "new covenant" through Christ, which grew out of the "old covenant" of the Jewish people with God, would naturally find its way into a body of written texts. So even as these first-century groups were going about the business of living out their new life in Christ, God was working to inspire and supply them with documents that would house His teaching and story, preserving it for generations to come.

2) WHAT SCRIPTURE REVEALS

- Three examples in the New Testament point to early knowledge among believers that Scripture was blooming before their eyes.

Call on a student to read 2 Peter 3:15-16.

Regard the patience of our Lord as an opportunity for salvation, just as our dear brother Paul has written to you according to the wisdom given to him. He speaks about these things in all his letters in which there are some matters that are hard to understand. The untaught and unstable twist them to their own destruction, as they also do *with the rest of the Scriptures.*

2 PETER 3:15–16 (emphasis added)

» **ASK:** What does the apostle Peter think about the writings of the apostle Paul? What does this tells us about how they viewed Paul's writings at that time?

- Point out to students that Peter's comments about Paul's writing was in passing, as if no one should be surprised to hear him mention Paul's letters on par with the Old Testament Scriptures.

Call on a student to read 1 Timothy 5:18

'Do not muzzle an ox while it is treading out the grain,' and, 'the worker is worthy of his wages.'

1 TIMOTHY 5:18

» **ASK:** Why is it significant that the Luke passage is paired with the passage in Deuteronomy?

- Point out that first-century Christians were already viewing Luke's Gospel, or at least some sayings of Jesus in it, in the same vein as Old Testament Scripture.

Call on a student to read 2 Peter 3:1-2.

Dear friends, this is now the second letter I have written to you; in both letters, I want to develop a genuine understanding with a reminder, so that you can remember the words previously spoken *by the holy prophets* and the command of our Lord and Savior *given through your apostles.*"

2 PETER 3:1–2, (emphasis added)

» **ASK:** How does this verse lend credit to the idea that the New Testament is as equally inspired as the Old Testament?

Answer the question using the following information:

"The holy prophets" and the "apostles." Old and New together—right there in the same sentence—showing that early in church history the complete canon was clearly coming together.

- In fact, by the end of the second century, the church father Irenaeus utilized a set of authoritative apostolic writings comprised of twenty of the eventual twenty-seven books of the New Testament, including a specific listing of the widely accepted four Gospels: Matthew, Mark, Luke, and John.[3]

- Another ancient document, the Muratorian Canon—most likely the earliest list of authoritative Christian books (around AD 180)—also affirms the four New Testament Gospels as being the only ones recognized as Scripture.[4]

Discuss the following information, emphasizing that most of the books of the New Testament were seen as authoritative Scripture long before the fourth-century councils.

» BOTTOM LINE

The historical evidence tells us that the thirteen letters of Paul, in short order with the Gospels and other writings of the apostles, were already being viewed as bearing the equal weight of Scripture.

» **STATE AND DISCUSS:** It is pretty clear from the historical evidence that the core canon of the New Testament appears to have been consistently sanctioned church-wide by at least the middle of the second century—long before any councils had obtained the political wherewithal to force heretical books out.

The establishment of the orthodox canon was hardly an "aha!" creation proposed by clever aides and advisors to the church council members of the fourth and later centuries. Actually, the canon was not even a point of discussion at those meetings! These gatherings were called for the purpose of clarifying theological issues (like who exactly is Jesus or how to define Trinity), and the only reason the canon came up at all was because these books were the ones the church leaders appealed to in defending their various arguments, opinions, and interpretations.

3) A SECOND FAILED OBJECTION

Discuss the following information.

Among the skeptical arguments you're likely to hear on this subject is how there's no way to distinguish between the books that were included in the New Testament and the writings that were excluded. According to some critics, the choice over which books to include was like a singing contest with subjective judges who already knew the ones they wanted to pick, despite the similar talents and worthiness of all contestants.

- However, the truth is, the books the skeptics want to call attention to don't even compare to the ones included in the New Testament canon. No one could have gotten away with forcing these books on the early believers or stuffing them into the accepted canon of Scripture.

  ≫ **ASK:** If you made something or had a business you wanted to promote, and could have anyone promote it for you and be the spokesperson, who would you pick, and why?

Discuss the following:

Think of it this way. When a Bible critic, like Bart Ehrman, releases a new book, he goes on a nationwide signing and speaking tour, hitting some of the big New York and California media, finding quick reception by the talent scheduler at Comedy Central who love having him on their talk shows. That's what you get when you write mega-best-selling books and can make a good appearance on camera.

But what about when some I.M. Nobody prints up his own scholarly volume through Publish-or-Perish Press—a book that's probably only been read by his mother, his editor, and maybe opened and closed for ten seconds by friends and colleagues who just need to tell him they've looked at it? Do you think the lines of people wanting to meet this author will wrap around the front windows of the bookstore? Do you think Oprah's returning his phone calls?

They want big names. They want big numbers. They want instant attachments to automatic success.

So when the PR-spinning creators of the Bible went looking for possible entries to include—the kind that would really impress the public, the kind that would put Christian belief on the map and force the world to pay attention—who would they want these books to be written by? Somebody like . . . Mark?

- Think about it. If the early church was going for instant punch and credibility by attributing their Gospels to heavy-hitting authors, why would they pick Mark when someone like Peter or Barnabas would have given them instant success? Mark couldn't hack the stress and strain on the road with Paul on his first missionary journey. Not only that, his desire for a second chance on a second trip created such a rift between major players Paul and Barnabas, they decided to split up and go their separate ways (see Acts 13:2–5, 13; 15:36–39). Why choose Mark when you have resumès from Peter and Barnabas at your disposal?

NAME	BACKGROUND
MARK	▸ Couldn't hack the stress and strain of traveling with Paul ▸ Left his first missionary journey ▸ Caused a rift between Paul and Barnabas
PETER	▸ Pre-eminent apostle and primary spokesman for the Twelve ▸ Key witness of events as Jesus' transfiguration ▸ Preached at Pentecost and saw over 3,000 saved
BARNABAS	▸ Known as the "son of encouragement" ▸ Generously gave field to the apostles ▸ Recruited Paul; commissioned by church to go with Paul on first missionary journey

Refer to the chart (on p. 28 of the student book) to see Mark's background contrasted with Peter's and Barnabas'.

"Hello, Mark. How'd you like to write a book for our new Bible?"

Never going to happen. It's well known now, and was well known then, in a tradition that reaches back to the early second century, that much of what Mark reported in his Gospel came from the preaching and eyewitness testimony of Peter. His first chapter records how Jesus called Peter away from his fishing business to follow him (Mark 1:16–18), and the last chapter records an angel telling the women who discovered the empty tomb, "Go, tell His disciples and Peter" to come meet up with the risen Christ (Mark 16:7).

How easy would it have been, if name recognition was the objective and if forgery was the plan, to drop Mark's involvement to the level of invisible ghostwriter and put Peter's name up there on the big, glossy book jacket? He was the natural choice. He was well known and highly regarded. He was an instant seller. Why then would tradition select Mark?

Because tradition must know something. Like that Mark was the one who wrote it. Just as Matthew wrote his Gospel. Just as Luke wrote his. John stands alone as the sole Gospel writer who truly brought high-level apostolic ambiance to the quartet. So we assure you, if the intention of the early church was merely to assign names to Gospel documents in hopes of investing them with greater authority, these rather obscure characters from the original crowd would not have been given top billing.

» GROUND RULES

Discuss the following, pointing out the three ground rules for authoritative Scripture:

It's really not as complicated as skeptical scholars and professors would lead you to assume. Most, if not all, of the New Testament documents were completed by the end of the first century. Though the process that resulted in the twenty-seven books of our canon was not initiated by a think tank or tested in a science lab, the general ground rules for accepting a book as authoritative boiled down to three characteristics. They had to have been:

A) written by an apostle or

B) by someone connected with an apostle, and

C) based on eyewitness, verifiable testimony.

» **ASK:** Why do you think this is the best criteria for determining which books to include?

When that last book of the Bible, Revelation, was written slightly before the turn of the first century, the New Testament was closed for all practical purposes. On the other hand, those pseudo books that critics always talk about were all written in the second and third centuries or later. And even if they could be magically transported back into the double-digit years of the first millennium, they still don't possess the gravitas to stand on the same platform with the established books of the New Testament. They never did.

It didn't take a church council to figure that out. It didn't take steel-toed intimidation to kick them out of the canon. The books of the biblical canon showed themselves to be special and came to be widely read and circulated over a vast region of the early church.

GROUP DISCUSSION

» 1) How and when were the books of the New Testament identified as Scripture?

» 2) What are some of the differences between the books of the New Testament and the books that were excluded?

≫ 3) What is some of the evidence used by critics to argue that parts of the New Testament were forged? How might you respond to their arguments?

CLOSING THOUGHTS

Discuss the closing thoughts to help summarize and reinforce the main points of this session.

Since the arguments from evil fail to overturn the Christian worldview, critics turn to other things to scrutinize, like the development of the Bible. Of course, being critical about how the Bible came to us is not bad so long as being critical means following the evidence where it leads. This is all we can ask of any reasonable person. We can say that because we are confident that any level-headed individual that isn't prejudiced from the start will arrive at the same historical conclusions we have throughout this session. Why? Because this is the best explanation of the historical evidence.

Thus, as we have seen, to question the origin of the Bible by denying its historicity and saying it is the product of those in power is completely without evidence. Instead, the evidence we do have all points to the historicity and valid origins of the Bible's composition.

By focusing on these truths, we accomplish at least two things:

≫ 1) We deepen our faith and trust in the historical roots and truthfulness of Scripture.

≫ 2) We provide for the critic a reasonable defense of our beliefs, as well as a counter-argument against the objections they raise.

APPLICATION

Remind students of the "head to heart to hand" model found in Session 1, then direct them to spend time reflecting/writing on how this session challenges them both inwardly and outwardly.

PERSONAL:

1) How has the information in this session strengthened your personal faith in God?

MISSIONAL:

2) How has the information in this session help prepare you to answer the skeptics and share with the unsaved?

CONTINUE THE STORY

Direct students to review the story found at the beginning of this session. Ask them how they would respond to Dan based upon what they have learned throughout this session?

SESSION 4

CONTRADICTIONS, CONTRADICTIONS

OPENING

Before the session, create a set of cards that contain oxymoron phrases, such as jumbo shrimp, alone together, civil war, crash landing, deafening silence, living dead, etc. Write the phrases on index cards, one phrase per card. Put all the cards into a bucket or paper bag. Divide students into two teams and play charades, using the oxymoron phrases. During each team's turn, one team member will act out a phrase while the rest of the team tries to guess the answer. The actor will get 15 seconds to look at the phrase, then 30 seconds to act it out. Play several rounds and give a small prize to the winning team. Debrief the game by explaining that all the phrases are oxymorons, a figure of speech formed by two words that are seemingly contradictory. Point out the contradictions in some of the phrases.

» **ASK:** Some people say the Bible has contradictions. Would you agree?

THE STORY

Kevin had been living with us for some time. He was our foreign exchange student, and he was a great kid. He was smart, funny, and always wanted to learn about our culture and traditions.

One Saturday afternoon we were sitting in the family room watching television. As I was flipping through the stations, a war movie including the battle of Pearl Harbor caught my eye. I always stop when movies like this come on, so I didn't think anything of it at the time. Soon Kevin began asking me questions about what war this was referring to, and the battle at Pearl Harbor in particular. After explaining the context of the movie, and a lot of what took place at Pearl Harbor, I'll always remember Kevin's reaction.

"That's not at all what happened," he said.

According to him and to what his home country had taught him, he grew up believing that Pearl Harbor was the fabricated story made by Americans in order to motivate the public to enter the war. He goes on to say that it was staged, and only one ship was sunk intentionally in order to propagate the lies.

If I thought Kevin's reaction was strong, I could only imagine what mine might have been. Knowing his background and where he was from, I came to realize that the best way to help him decide between these two contradictory accounts of Pearl Harbor would be to help him discover the historical evidences that are available. After all, I was pretty confident that historical evidences would win out on this one.

THE QUESTION

Call on a student to read the question for the session:
Does the Bible contain contradictions?

FIRST RESPONSE

» **ASK:** If you had to answer that question today, how would you respond?

THE SKEPTIC'S VIEW

Discuss the skeptic's view of this issue using the information below.

There are critics out there who claim that the Bible is "full of contradictions." For most of these critics, asking them to supply you with one of these so-called contradictions would likely cause them great embarrassment on account that they don't know of any—they only heard someone else say it. Instead of considering the evidence for themselves, they have simply followed some questionable authority figure blindly without personally checking the facts. This type of situation happens more often than you think—someone hears something on a television program or thinks it must be true because his college professor said it. It is a pity when this happens.

But what about those that do claim to have an example or two? For them, any sort of literary diversity or historical development equals internal disagreement and contradiction. It seems that anything shy of word-for-word agreement entails contradictory accounts. But is this true? How should we answer them? Are there real contradictions, or does the Bible display a remarkable unity among its development? How would you respond when faced with this reaction?

Hopefully by the end of this session we will be in agreement with biblical scholar Ben Witherington III when he said:

"The more I studied the Bible, the less I was prone to accuse the Bible of obvious historical errors and stupid mistakes, including theological errors about a matter as profound as human suffering and evil. To the contrary, I found the Bible rich, complex, varied, and helpful and truthful in dealing with precisely such life and death matters....In my case, my faith in the Bible was strengthened..."

THE RESPONSE

1) UNDERSTANDING CONTRADICTIONS

First, what is a contradiction? A contradiction is a combination of words and/or ideas that are opposed to one another.

» ASK: An example of a contradiction would be a square circle, or a married bachelor. Can you think of any more contradictions?

» ASK: Is every perceived contradiction a real contradiction?

» ASK: Does difference really equal contradiction as some claim?

Use the following illustration to help students understand the difference between diversity and disagreement.

Suppose you're sitting around with a bunch of friends, maybe at a restaurant or some other place; and in the flow of conversation, you start telling a story about something you did or saw and the way you remember it. Halfway through, one of your other friends—who was also there and saw the same thing—jumps in and adds an extra detail or two that you'd forgotten or left out. This goes on, back and forth, with maybe other friends occasionally interrupting, laying down a third or fourth perspective on a shared experience.

» ASK: Would you call that diversity or disagreement?

What's happening here? Since you're not all saying the same words or describing events in exactly the same way, are all but one of you lying? or confused? or being intentionally deceptive? Based on these differences in what you're saying, are you obviously contradicting one another?

Or wouldn't it be much fairer to acknowledge, by contrast, that a person sitting there listening to each of you talk would actually get a much more complete, more interesting, more well-rounded picture of the memory you're all describing?

> **ASK:** Why would a story retold in this way, with no contradictions, be more compelling than a group of people recounting an event word-for-word?

> **STATE AND DISCUSS:** "Diversity doesn't necessarily mean disagreement."

The Bible is like the friends retelling the story. Instead of the various accounts of Scripture revealing a lack of unity in the overall message, their individual works actually weave a tapestry that's much more compelling and less monochromatic than some one-note, robotic printout or press release.

- The Bible is not like a government document, processed in triplicate. No, it's living and breathing. It's layered and textured. It's God's work in real life, in the real world, with real people, living in a real time, not a carefully managed sheet of talking points designed to keep any of its writers from going off message.

> **STATE AND DISCUSS:** "When you think about it, actually, the variety of perspectives found in the Bible—far from being a threat to the divine inspiration of Scripture—are part of what proves its validity."

If some critics weren't trying so hard to impose a rigid, artificial structure onto the way God should have written His book (if they'd been in charge of things), they might find some highly plausible reasons for why any of these so-called inconsistencies are really among its greatest assets.

- What you'll see, we believe, is that the statements of these various biblical writers are, yes, diverse across time and personalities, but not in disagreement across the board. And that means they're not contradictions.

2) UNDERSTANDING DIVERSITY WITHIN SCRIPTURE

Perhaps you've been reeled in before by the gavel-to-gavel television coverage of a high- profile courtroom case. The prosecution lays out their version of what happened; then the defense counters with their own testimony and witnesses. And by the time the jury is sent back to chambers to arrive at a verdict, their job is to what? It's to see if they can gather up all the information they've heard and piece it back together into a smooth, single, comprehensive flow of events.

What are they doing? Answer: they're harmonizing the material. That's because no one individual who took the witness stand told every detail, start to finish, of the whole series of circumstances involved in the case. But in the end, by laying everything on top of everything else, the jury works with all the stray bits of evidence to craft a reasonable time line and to recreate in their mind the big picture.

>> ASK: How does harmonizing apply to anything we know about the past? How do you imagine that works with events like World War II, the Civil War, or the American Revolution?

Historians do this all the time. When dealing with ancient history, they're basically forced to. They'll read dozens, perhaps hundreds of books, articles, and samples of written correspondence; they'll listen to tapes and lectures and personal interviews; they'll research as many accounts as they can find on whatever subject they're seeking to capture: a war, a time period, a movement, a presidency. Then finally, ultimately, they're able to present a pieced-together summary of what they believe happened, in what order, all in relation to what other things were going on at the same time.

>> ASK: If harmonizing past events is important for understanding them correctly, shouldn't we also apply them to biblical events? Explain why this would be important.

>> STATE AND DISCUSS: "Now some people don't think the Bible—if it had been written the way it was supposed to—should require harmonization. If it's inspired by God, the details should be abundantly clear, without any question or suspicion to be sorted out."

>> ASK: Do you agree with this statement? Why or why not?

- People that think this way also think that if they had been in charge of writing the Bible, they sure would've done a better job of keeping it perfectly consistent in every place. Seems like that's something God should be able to do.

When people make this type of argument, it's designed to rattle your cage and make you feel like you've caught God in an awkward, weakened position. But this whole line of thought is curious, considering that harmonization is so standard a practice among historians and considering how long ago the events of Scripture took place. Apparently what's acceptable for studying Alexander the Great, Julius Caesar, Mozart, or Babe Ruth just doesn't get to apply to Jesus and the Bible. Just because.

3) A TEST CASE

The level-headed thinker, however, will apply the same historical practices for evaluating so-called "contradictions" in Scripture that deal with time lines—descriptions of what happened when, what happened first, what happened next. Why doesn't it always sound the same? Why aren't events always presented in the same order?

Instruct students to read LUKE 23:44-46, MATTHEW 27:50, **and** MARK 15:37-39, **and look for the discrepancy in these accounts.**

Ancient literature from the period of the gospels was consistently less worried about putting things in chronological order than arranging them by theme and topic. That's just a fact. So, for example, when Luke reported the tearing of the temple veil before Jesus' death (LUKE 23:44–46) and Matthew and Mark mentioned it after Jesus' death (MATTHEW 27:50; MARK 15:37–39), there's a pretty simple reason for the rearrangement.

According to ceremonial law, the heavily embroidered curtain they were referencing separated the holy of holies from the rest of the inner temple (2 CHRONICLES 3:14), signifying a place that was accessible only to the high priest, and then only once a year on the Day of Atonement (HEBREWS 6:7). So this rending of the temple veil that coincided with Jesus' crucifixion—"split in two from top to bottom" (MATTHEW 27:51)—was keenly symbolic of what his death meant: the removal of all barriers between man and God. It was an epic, illustrative miracle.

Matthew and Luke, being much more descriptive than Mark, chose to group this amazing wonder alongside some of the other cosmic signs that occurred on that momentous day—the midnight darkness at noontime, the rumble of a rock-splitting earthquake, resurrected bodies emerging from their opened tombs—presenting these events in no particular order. The added weight of sorting them out chronologically resonates more with the mind-set of our modern thinking. That's the way we typically process events today when we retell and research them. But we're being a bit arrogant and unforgiving to force our linear perspectives onto writers of earlier times who just weren't as accustomed to orienting their histories in that fashion. These writers weren't lying. They and their original readers and hearers just weren't always hung up on the same things that preoccupy us today.

» ASK: How does this example show diversity but not disagreement?

One simply chose to present the detail as part of another theme they saw as more relevant than giving chronology. And as writers they have the right to make those choices. Just like in a courtroom, a few loose ends can pop up where the pieces don't exactly fit together. But in case after case in Scripture, as seen in the example above, solid arguments can be made for why they appear the way they do.

4) A HELPFUL ANALOGY

- Some people who champion the freedom of diversity will not tolerate the presence of diversity in the Bible. Some people who accuse Christianity of being so off-key will not allow the Bible to harmonize its way into cohesion. And some people who think we're ridiculously foolish to hold onto our faith are perhaps too slow to allow us the common courtesy of using our common sense.

» ASK: If you could go on a tour with a band, which one would you pick, and why would you pick them?

Share the following analogy to help explain the point.

Just for a moment let's assume you're an avid follower of a certain band or musical performer, you might be tempted one year (if you had the time and money) to take in as many as three or four of their concerts on whatever tour they were doing. You saw them in Nashville, in Atlanta, in Orlando, and even once in California, a lot farther away from home. No doubt you detected a good bit of scripting in the various performances you saw. The song order was a lot the same. Some of the same jokes and one-liners appeared at the same part of the show. But because you became so familiar with the general flow of the evening, you particularly noticed when they would personalize their banter for the local crowd—"Hello, Chicago! How 'bout them Cubs?"—or when they reconfigured their set of material slightly from one of the previous concerts you'd seen. You would actually have been disappointed, to tell you the truth, if being there in person had been like listening to the exact same "live" recording every single time.

The harshest skeptics are often guilty of treating the biblical account of Jesus' life as if it's a series of "one night only" events and that whatever He might have said, done, or taught in one town or one setting comprised the only time He ever said, did, or taught those particular things. And so if we ever hear one of the Gospels use a different word from another Gospel in recalling something Jesus said, then the Bible is obviously misquoting Him.

- However, Jesus certainly would have spoken on certain topics more than once, and in different venues. (Remember: He was a traveling preacher.) It's not like people could check Jesus' Twitter feed or the local news. Would His every appearance in every town include nothing but all-new material? And did He possess so little personality or awareness of each audience that He never varied his delivery from place to place?

Like any good teacher, wouldn't He have taught often by repetition, reinforcing His intended principles, giving them more opportunities to stick in His listeners' heads and hearts? Might He react to a real-time event by stating a previously spoken truth but cast it in a way that matched the situation? Of course. Logic.

>> **STATE AND DISCUSS:** "The early church viewed the diversity of the New Testament documents as an advantage rather than a liability. They understood that four distinct, historical sources proved much more helpful in giving a richer portrait of Christ than any one source ever could, no matter how detailed."

>> **ASK:** Does this statement make sense to you? Explain.

GROUP DISCUSSION

>> 1) What is the difference between legitimate diversity and contradiction?

>> 2) Have you ever had a particular experience with a friend in which you recounted the

story in different ways? Was it a matter of one of you getting the facts wrong, or did you just tell the story in different ways?

» 3) How might Jesus' itinerant ministry (He traveled around preaching to different groups) have led to some of the differences we see in the Gospels?

» 4) How does diversity lend itself to the trustworthiness of Scripture?

CLOSING THOUGHTS

Discuss the closing thoughts to help summarize and reinforce the main points of this session.

The argument that diversity within the Bible equals disagreement and/or contradiction is clearly false. As we have learned, if every report of the gospels, for instance, were word-for-word the same, we would likely have a hard believing that these were written independently of one another – it's the equivalent of Johnny and James turning in the same book report in eight grade English class while continuing to claim that they didn't work together. However, given the diversity we do have, and how this diversity displays a remarkable unity to the person and work of Jesus, Christians should be all the more confident that Scripture's testimony is true.

By focusing on these truths, we accomplish at least two things:

» 1) We strengthen our own faith and trust in the truthfulness and reliability of Scripture.

» 2) We provide for the critic a reasonable defense of how diversity doesn't entail contradiction, but instead counts towards the Bible's credibility.

APPLICATION

Remind students of the "head to heart to hand" model found in Session 1, then direct them to spend time reflecting/writing on how this session challenges them both inwardly and outwardly.

PERSONAL:

1) **How has the information in this session strengthened your personal faith in God?**

MISSIONAL:

2) **How has the information in this session help prepare you to answer the skeptics and share with the unsaved?**

CONTINUE THE STORY

Direct students to review the story at the beginning of the session. Ask them how they would respond to someone who was criticizing the Bible, saying it was full of contradictions, based upon what they have learned throughout this session?

SESSION 5

I'LL NEED AN ORIGINAL

OPENING

Play a game of "Two Truths and a Lie" with your students. Distribute index cards and instruct students to write three statements about themselves on the card. Two of the statements need to be little-known facts, the other statement needs to be a lie. After everyone has written their "facts," instruct one student at a time to read his or her statements. Make sure students read their statements in random order. The other students discuss and try to determine which statement is a lie. Allow all or most students to read their cards, then debrief with these questions:

> **ASK:** How easy was it to determine which statement was a lie? What tipped you off?

THE STORY

There I was, sitting in my senior year of high school literature, enjoying our discussion of Old Testament literature. Although I was enjoying learning about the different genres and literary devices of the Old Testament, I was somewhat shocked to learn that the Bible would be our object of study in the public school I was attending.

A few days after we began our study, one of my classmates asked the teacher whether the narratives and histories we were reading in the Old Testament had been altered since their writing. Without hesitation, the teacher emphatically said, "Of course they have!" He went on to say to the class that "even though we are studying the literature of the Bible, we should keep in mind that the Bible has evolved throughout the centuries, having been altered and changed to suit different purposes."

» THE QUESTION

Call on a student to read the question for the session:

Are our Bibles the same as the original manuscripts?

FIRST RESPONSE

» **ASK:** If you had to answer that question today, how would you respond?

THE SKEPTIC'S VIEW

Discuss the skeptic's view of this issue using the information below.

As we all know, the Bible was not written in English and photocopied down throughout the centuries. In fact, none of the originals—that is, the actual original copies that Matthew, Mark, and Paul wrote, for instance, are still around today. In light of this, some Bible critics argue that the Bible we know today is different from the original, having been changed and modified over the years on account of scribal error or, much worse, intentional tampering. For instance, Bart Ehrman says, "One of the things that people misunderstand, of course—especially my nineteen-year-old students from North Carolina—is that when we're reading the Bible, we're not actually reading the words of Matthew, Mark, Luke, John, or Paul. We're reading translations of the originals of Matthew, Mark, Luke, John, or Paul, because we don't have the originals of any of the books of the New Testament."

But is this true? Does it necessarily follow that we can't know what the originals said because we don't have the originals? Not hardly. As we will see throughout this lesson, all of the evidence that we do have supports the belief that we do know what the originals said, contrary to what the Bible critics would say.

▸ So, how do we respond to such charges? What evidence is there to support the belief that the words of Scripture we have today are accurate reflections of the original documents? How would you respond if ever presented with this accusation?

THE RESPONSE

1) A BRIEF GLANCE AT ANCIENT DOCUMENTS

» **ASK:** Why would it be important to have as many early copies as possible of an old book?

» **ASK:** How many copies from older works do you think historians usually work with?

▸ To begin developing a response to this point of view, let's start by looking at ancient literature in general. The only way people know of any ancient literature is by way of copies, not originals. That's not only true of the Bible; it's true of virtually everything else. And because we're dealing with writings that are so extremely old, you can imagine how few of these manuscripts are likely to have survived into modern times.

Point out the illustration on page 45 in the student book that shows the number of surviving manuscripts for some historical documents.

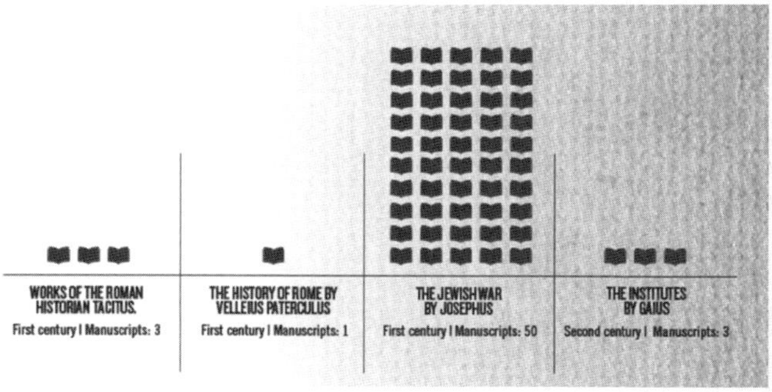

▸ This illustration shows four well-known works from antiquity, including the approximate date of their writing and the number of manuscripts currently on hand.
▸ Notice that Josephus has by far the most at 50. That number is fairly unusual for writings this old.
▸ In almost every case even the most widely accepted works from ancient philosophers and historians are considered verifiable with only a small handful of available sources to vouch for them.

» **ASK:** How many early copies of the New Testament do you think we have?

We'll give you a hint: it's way more than fifty. Try more like fifty-eight hundred. And if you add Latin, you have over eight thousand more.

And that doesn't include a vast number of citations—places where Christian teachers of the first centuries A.D., quoting directly from Scripture in their own writings, provide even more evidence of what the earliest documents of the Bible actually said. Even Bible critics have admitted that if all of these secondhand quotes were compiled and cataloged in biblical order, laid from end to end, they would be "sufficient alone for the reconstruction of practically the entire New Testament."[5]

» **ASK:** How does that lend credibility to the Scriptures?

» **STATE AND DISCUSS:** The Bible is by far the best-attested book of ancient origin.

2) WHAT DO DATES HAVE TO DO WITH IT?

» **ASK:** Why is earlier the better when it comes to copies of the Scriptures?

So, going back to our question, how do you answer claims that the Bible is so full of everything from typos to intentional tampering that we can't trust it? Is it possible, even if you're not able to produce an original document with the original information written by the original author, you can still know what the original said with reasonable certainty?

- Imagine your mom called to you from the kitchen one evening and said to go tell your little brother and sister, that supper will be ready in fifteen minutes, that one of them needs to set the table and the other one needs to put ice in the glasses. So you get up from whatever you're doing, you walk upstairs, you stand in the hallway where they can both hear you in their rooms, and you say, "Hey, guys, Mom says supper is in fifteen minutes. She wants one of you to set the table and one of you to put ice in the glasses."

All right, did your mom give them these instructions herself? No.

But is that what your mom told you to tell them? Yes.

- Ask the younger siblings in this little example. And see if everybody doesn't come down for supper.

Remember back when we were talking just a few minutes ago about the number of manuscripts that have been preserved from ancient literature? Another way to look at this data is to try determining how old the surviving copies are and then subtract their distance in years (or centuries) from when the originals were thought to have been written. The smaller the chronological gap, you'd think, between original and earliest known copy, the higher the likelihood that the first manuscript in our possession reflects what was originally said. Make sense?

Point out the timeline in the student book that shows the oldest manuscripts on file, and then subtract to determine how far apart these copies are from the original.

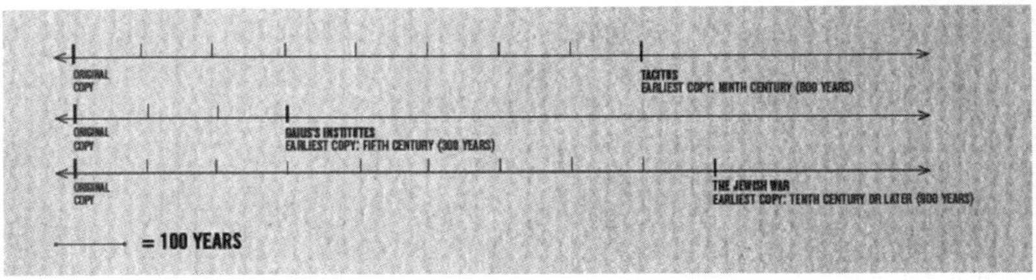

- Tacitus. Earliest copy: ninth century (800 years after originally written)
- Gaius's Institutes. Earliest copy: fifth century (300 years)
- The Jewish War. Earliest copy: tenth century or later (900 years)

See the customary time gap we're dealing with? Eight hundred years, nine hundred years—three hundred at the extreme outside.

- An important thing to remember is that when it comes to these other works, ancient historians work with these copies and discuss history based on their wording. Despite how few manuscripts we have and how large the gap is we still work with these texts. And yet when we get around to the Bible, not only does it far outweigh everything else on the manuscript count—by hundreds and thousands—it also blows away this test on chronological spacing as well.

The New Testament was written, most scholars agree, between A.D. 50 (if not earlier, in the case of the book of James) and about A.D. 100 (Revelation). And our earliest fragment—the John Rylands Papyrus—is a portion of John's Gospel which dates from approximately A.D. 125.

That's hardly a generation later. Twenty or thirty years. Compared to gaping hundreds! And what's more, by the second, third, and fourth centuries, the number of verifiable biblical manuscripts just explodes. Whole sections. Whole books.

Again, the wealth of available material is not even in the same league as other writings from that period. Nowhere close.

» **ASK:** How does knowing the distance of time between when the originals were written to the time of our earliest copies increase your confidence in the Bible?

- These many and early ancient Scripture texts are far, far greater than the sample size of any comparable writing from that era.
- The many available manuscripts, standing at such close proximity to the originals, offer a windfall of material that scholars who study other ancient works would love to have.

»THE NEXT BEST THING

If they can't have the original, what they want are as many manuscripts as possible so they can compare readings and look for both consistencies and inconsistencies, helping them deduce what the original almost certainly said. And nothing does that like the ancient records of Scripture.

- So when you consider the large amount of biblical copying that was being done at the time, as well as the close proximity between the original writings (known as autographs) and the earliest known manuscripts, why are we forced to conclude that the copies are so measurably different from where they started? Or that they're any different at all?

» **STATE AND DISCUSS:** So when scholars assert the likelihood of wholesale changes of a now lost original, they're making what's known as an argument from silence—not an appeal to proof and reason and historical documentation but just an imaginary game of connect-the-dots—with no dots and no pencil.

- It takes a massive leap to get there. This view is unduly skeptical. Without the original, there's no undeniable evidence that the Scriptures have been altered.

The best check is in the manuscripts we do have.

- With all these copies to work from, and with their nearness to the approximate date of authorship, the most likely conclusion is this: even with a number of changes embedded here and there within the various manuscripts—whether by mistake or by intention—the original wording is still present within the full body of material.

Share this analogy to reinforce the importance of earliest copies of manuscripts.

Think of it this way. If you were to make fifty photocopies of this page you're reading right now, and you gave one each to fifty different people, along with a Sharpie pen and these instructions: Cross out one word on each page—any word—and give the sheet back to me. By the time you reassembled all fifty pages, what are the chances that the same word would have been marked through fifty times by fifty people? Almost none, right? The most logical hypothesis would say that every single word on these two pages would still be discoverable by comparing all fifty of these slightly marred papers against the others.

That's how you get back to the original—even with mistakes potentially present in all the manuscripts individually. And that's why the more manuscripts you can access, the greater your confidence that you can locate the original wording. Otherwise, it's like the old joke that says if you have two watches, you don't really know for sure what time it is. The chances of both of them being on the same minute and second at the same moment is pretty slight. But if you had a hundred watches, a thousand watches—fifty-eight hundred watches—you could get really, really close to the exact time. If not right on it.

4) TEXTUAL CRITICISM

This is the kind of work that's done by an entire field of research and study we already identified as textual criticism.[6] You're likely to hear this term a lot in your college courses on the Bible and religion, as well as in PBS documentaries and *TIME* magazine articles.

Explain the job of a biblical text critic:

Analyzes the unusual wealth of ancient information to try to determine, by comparing the available materials against one another, what the original documents of Scripture most likely said.

As a result, with all these manuscripts to work from, what we have is not a loss of the original but just a thin, added layer of inconsistencies—differences in wording or spelling or sentence structure—what scholars refer to as variants. In other words we have too much of the text, not too little, to sift out the authentic from the unauthentic. We might even say that instead of having less than 100 percent of the Bible text, we have more like 105 percent. We haven't completely lost the original portion; to the contrary, it is more reasonable to conclude that we have the original and then a little more. It just takes a little dusting and sweeping to clean up the extra scraps and get it back like it was.

Possessing more manuscripts of ancient literature should be nothing but a positive. Never a negative. Any fair-minded historian would agree with that. Only an excessive skepticism turns a benefit into a problem. That move is neither necessary nor reasonable.

GROUP DISCUSSION

» 1) How can we reasonably support the belief that our Bible matches the original text of Scripture?

» 2) How do scholars determine the original words of the New Testament?

» 3) How does the New Testament manuscript evidence compare to the evidence for other books written in the first century?

» 4) How do we accoundt for the differences in the manuscripts of the New Testament?

» 5) Can anyone prove we do not have the original words of the New Testament? Why or why not?

CLOSING THOUGHTS

Discuss the closing thoughts to help summarize and reinforce the main points of this session.

Even though skeptics have questioned the accuracy of today's Bible based on the fact that none of the first documents exist, we have seen that the absence of these originals in no way shatters our belief that the Bible has been faithfully preserved throughout the centuries. A large part of this confidence stems from the facts that 1) we have several thousand copies of just the New Testament alone (not to mention the Old Testament) to compare with, and 2) the fact that the ones we do have are close in date to the time the originals were written. As we have seen, the Bible, unlike any other historic document, is quite unique in this sense.

By focusing on these truths, we accomplish at least two things:

» 1) We settle our own fears about the preservation of God's Word throughout the centuries, and

» 2) We provide an extremely defensive argument against the critic by showing their position to be without reasonable support or evidence.

APPLICATION

Remind students of the "head to heart to hand" model found in Session 1, then direct them to spend time reflecting/writing on how this session challenges them both inwardly and outwardly.

PERSONAL

1) How has the information in this session strengthened you personal faith in God?

MISSIONAL

2) How has the information in this session help prepare you to answer the skeptics and share with the unsaved?

CONTINUE THE STORY

Direct students to review the story found at the beginning of this session. Ask them how they would respond to a friend who was questioning how the Bible was formed, based upon what they have learned throughout this session?

SESSION 6

AND THE WINNER IS . . .

OPENING

Provide paper for the students and explain that you are going to give them a pop quiz on the life of Jesus. Ask the following questions, then check students answers. (Answers in bold.)

1) Which of the following animals were at the manger when Jesus was born?
   a) Cows, sheep & camels b) sheep & pigs c) only sheep **d) we don't know**

2) Who of the following was not one of the original 12 disciples of Jesus?
   a) Matthew b) Nathaniel **c) Luke** d) John

3) What was Jesus profession before He began His public ministry?
   a) tentmaker **b) carpenter** c) fisherman d) shepherd

4) Which is not one of Jesus' recorded miracles?
   a) raising the dead b) calming the storm c) casting out demons
   d) making the sun stand still

5) Which of the following stories is not one of Jesus' parables:
a) Prodigal Son **b) Trojan Horse** c) Good Samaritan
d) Wheat and Tares

6) Who betrayed Jesus?
a) Judas b) Peter c) Paul d) Matthew

7) Who did Pilate release to the people instead of Jesus?
a) Barnabas b) Bartholomew **c) Barabbas** d)Barney

» **ASK:** Did you get confused with any of the questions? How did you know the right answers? How do you know they are right? How do you think one of your unchurched friends would have done on the test?

THE STORY

I got a part-time job working at the local mall during my senior year of high school. Just across from the kiosk where I worked was another small kiosk owned and operated by two brothers.

I introduced myself to them not long after beginning my job. We often chatted when both businesses were slow. After a while, I realized they were both Muslim. They also knew that I was a Christian, since the topic of religion came up pretty frequently.

I remember one particular day I asked one of the brothers specifically what he thought about Jesus. Who is He? He said that "for Muslims, Jesus was a prophet. He was an important prophet, but a prophet only – he was a man."

I followed up by asking him whether he thought his view was an accurate portrayal of Jesus as found in the Gospels and the rest of the New Testament? He responded by saying "no," and then went on to add that "the teaching of the New Testament was made up by a group of people who tried to get everyone to believe their version of who Jesus was."

After hearing that, my next question should have been a simple one for him. "What historical evidence do you have to support that conclusion?"

THE QUESTION

Call on a student to read the question for the session:
Do the stories in the New Testament reflect what actually happened, or are they fictitious?

FIRST RESPONSE

» **ASK:** If you had to answer that question today, how would you respond?

THE SKEPTIC'S VIEW

Discuss the skeptic's view of this issue using the information below.

For him and many others, the version of Christianity that is so well known today in the Gospels is a version that not only misrepresents the historic Jesus, but is also the one that essentially won out among a number of competing versions. To hear them talk, it was sort of like March Madness back in the early centuries, a free-for-all, ongoing battles between opposing teams, beating up on each other through the brackets, until one stood alone in that "one shining moment," tearing down the nets of victory. We win! Take that!

The skeptic will say that the reason Christianity looks the way it does today, the reason the Bible teaches what it does, the reason we sit in our churches on Sunday and call this particular brand of belief "Christian faith" is only because this is the side that won. It could have just as easily gone another direction.

But the question remains: Is this what God's people have always believed? Has there always been one true and authentic Christian story, and is that what we have in our Bibles today? This chapter you're about to read goes back in time to show you the skeptic's argument is simply not the case by painting a picture of what the faith traditions of your church and the early church had in common. After all, it's important to know whether our Christian faith has always been the Christian faith.

THE RESPONSE

1) WERE THERE MULTIPLE COMPETING STORIES?

» **ASK:** Have you ever heard two different versions of an event that took place? How did you go about determining which version was correct?

The cynical belief that there were multiple early traditions competing to be number one owes more to ideological prejudice than to responsible, verifiable research. For them, the Bible rose up in later centuries, declared itself the Christian right, and said everybody else was wrong—when the only thing anybody else wanted was just to get along.

Instruct students to read Galatians 1:6; 1 Timothy 1:3; Titus 1:5.

» **ASK:** Based on these verses, did the early church experience controversy with false teaching? Why do you think God made sure this was included in His Word?

No one disputes that Christianity was filled with controversies in its early days (or still today, for that matter). Theological wildfires are nothing new. But most of the controversies the apostles were addressing in the first century—disputes such as whether circumcision was required of Gentile believers—do not touch on the core debates of orthodoxy that would later arise.[7] In other words, the big debates didn't take place right off the bat.

When you hear a critic or television program talk about one of these dissenting groups, they are referring to groups that came up centuries later after Christianity was already established. Most of these groups cannot be dated from historical sources before the second century. Just can't.[8] We have no evidence to support the argument that all of this significant diversity was happening right off the bat.

- The evidence shows orthodoxy as being pervasive and stable throughout the second, third, and fourth centuries.[9] Consistently. Across continents.

>> **ASK:** Why do you think it works in the Christian's favor in knowing that Christianity's core beliefs were settled for a long time before false teaching began?

- But if, for argument's sake, we were to concede the widespread, burgeoning, equal presence of Christian factions during these later centuries—seeing them almost like our current choice between Methodists, Baptists, and Presbyterians—nothing but pure conjecture can place them at or near the dawn of the early church. And nothing but wishful thinking can portray them as robust alternatives to authentic faith and belief. [10]

2) A GNOSTIC EXAMPLE

- To see what we are saying here, take Gnosticism, for example, which clearly posed the greatest threat to Christianity. If any heresy should have been high on the watch list, it was this one.

Gnosticism can only be construed as a broad label that covered a wide variety of groups with wildly divergent views. As a general rule Gnostics:

1) were highly suspicious of all things physical, including the humanity of Jesus.
2) held to the presence of a secret mystical knowledge that set them above the everyday crowd.
3) never developed any organization or unity.
4) supported a teaching that rejected the Old Testament.

How did Christianity compare with Gnositicism? Christianity:

1) began planting flourishing churches as early as the A.D. 40s and 50s.[11]
2) maintained core beliefs, as seen in the New Testament documents, which were written mid-first century.
3) stressed the importance of holding on to true doctrine and rejecting false teaching. It's hard to read the letters of Paul, for instance, and not see a clear, early body of orthodox beliefs that were up and operational from the get-go.

By the second century this "rule of faith" had successfully bridged the gap between the ministry of the apostles and those who emerged as leaders heading into the next generation—

the church fathers. They saw themselves as "handing down" what had been entrusted to them by those who had actually walked with Christ.

More than that, the church fathers understood their doctrine as being rooted in the Jewish Scriptures—the Old Testament—tying the church to the truly ancient faith of God's people and the prophetic messages that were fulfilled in Christ and proclaimed by the apostles. They weren't inventing a rule of faith; they were recipients of it.

» **STATE AND DISCUSS:** "Their writings reveal an awareness and affirmation of a commonly held faith, a theological standard that unified a geographically diverse group of post-New Testament churches."[12]

» **ASK:** Why is a commonly held faith and a unified theological standard so important?

The battle for Christianity's public face was not a tug-of-war among equals. These opponents did produce enough of a stir to worry orthodox writers for a time. But they eventually faded away, in part because of the endorsement of social and political forces Constantine launched in the fourth century, but also because they lacked the early and strong roots that orthodoxy had.

» **STATE AND DISCUSS:** "Those in the early church weren't clinging to Christ in hopes of attaining social or political power. They did it because they believed this teaching to be true. Because it was true. Is true."

» **ASK:** Why do you cling to Christ? Do you follow Him to be popular or embellish your image? Or do you follow Him because you believe He is the truth, the only way? Explain.

- It wasn't until much later—A.D. 313, with the sanctioning of the Edict of Milan by Emperor Constantine—that Christians acquired the official means to take action against heretical groups. And by this time Gnosticism had already faded quietly from the scene, all on its own, vanishing into the thin air their beliefs were anchored in, long before orthodox Christianity could pop the balloon for them.

» **ASK:** So when we take a view of the second-, third-, and fourth-century world and see Christian orthodoxy thriving and see heresies like Gnosticism sputtering, what does that tell you? Who was most likely the parasite of whom? Amid all this apparent (or imagined) diversity, who was marching boldly ahead, and who was off to the side?

3) SCRIPTURAL AFFIRMATION

According to the critics of Christianity, the centuries between Christ's ascension and the official construction of the Bible are just a mess of different thinking and beliefs. But that's not the evidence that Scripture presents.

Group students into teams. Instruct them to read the following passages and note how the following passages define understandings about Jesus, his identity and mission, and His purpose for the church.

MATTHEW 16:16-18; 28:18-20
ACTS 2:42
GALATIANS 1:6-9, 11-12
2 THESSALONIANS 2:15
ROMANS 1:2-4; 16:17
COLOSSIANS 1:15-20
PHILIPPIANS 2:6-11
2 TIMOTHY 1:13-14
JUDE 3
1 JOHN 4:1-2

- The New Testament paints a much different portrait than those who say early Christianity lacked benchmarks for how to weed out true teaching from false teaching. Note from these passages:
  - The apostles knew their mission was to pass on Jesus' message to subsequent generations.
  - The church understood the importance of being faithful to the apostles' teaching.
  - The core message of the gospel was tied to the nature and work of Christ.

4) A BIRD'S EYE VIEW

Bible skeptics insist on imposing an artificially murky distance between the life of Jesus and the establishment of the Christian faith. But let's take a little stroll from the first century to the fourth, noting the ongoing connections from one season to the next. The following exercise serves as an approximate outline of the relationship between orthodoxy and divergent forms of heresy in the first three hundred years of Christianity.[13]

Walk through the diagram with the students, noting the events that took place in each timeframe.

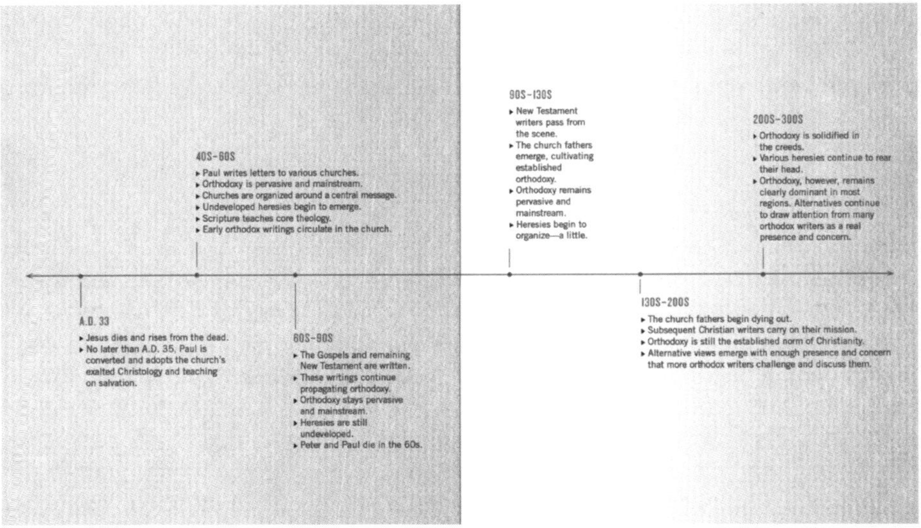

A.D. 33

- Jesus dies and rises from the dead.
- No later than A.D. 35, Paul is converted and adopts the church's exalted Christology and teaching on salvation.

40S–60s

- Paul writes letters to various churches.
- Orthodoxy is pervasive and mainstream.
- Churches are organized around a central message.
- Undeveloped heresies begin to emerge.
- Scripture teaches core theology.
- Early orthodox writings circulate in the church.

60S–90s

- The Gospels and remaining New Testament are written.
- These writings continue propagating orthodoxy.
- Orthodoxy stays pervasive and mainstream.
- Heresies are still undeveloped.
- Peter and Paul die in the 60s.

90S–130s

- New Testament writers pass from the scene.
- The church fathers emerge, cultivating established orthodoxy.
- Orthodoxy remains pervasive and mainstream.
- Heresies begin to organize—a little.

130S–200s

- The church fathers begin dying out.
- Subsequent Christian writers carry on their mission.
- Orthodoxy is still the established norm of Christianity.
- Alternative views emerge with enough presence and concern that more orthodox writers challenge and discuss them.

200S–300s

- Orthodoxy is solidified in the creeds.
- Various heresies continue to rear their head.
- Orthodoxy, however, remains clearly dominant in most regions. Alternatives continue to draw attention from many orthodox writers as a real presence and concern.

And we'll stop there. As you can see, the A.D. 300s did witness a significant moment in how Christian orthodoxy was defined. But only in a technical sense, not in a material sense—not in a way that changed or radicalized the orthodox teaching that had been in force from the founding of the early church. This is where skeptics make too much of their arguments, implying that orthodoxy was cobbled together late in the game just to crush the opposition. Are there still rivals to orthodox belief today? Yes. People who want to tack Jesus onto heresy?

Yes. False teaching? Yes. And the church is commissioned even now, just as it was in its earliest days, to address and expose error, "holding to the faithful message as taught . . . to encourage with sound teaching and to refute those who contradict it" (TITUS 1:9).

GROUP DISCUSSION

» 1) What are some ways the present culture prizes diversity?

» 2) When is a culture's love for diversity a positive, and when is it a problem for those who believe in absolute truth?

» 3) How do the passages cited in this chapter imply that the early church was careful to distinguish between true and false beliefs?

» 4) How has this lesson addressed any personal questions you have struggled with?

CLOSING THOUGHTS

Discuss the closing thoughts to summarize and reinforce the main points of this session.

The critic would have us believe that the stories we read throughout the New Testament are simply the ones that won out among a long list of competitors. For whatever reason—perhaps because of popularity, or a power play—the stories themselves were selected for a reason besides their historical truthfulness. However, as we've demonstrated throughout this lesson, that argument simply doesn't stand. Even a surface glance of our historical evidence shows not only that the stories contained are not only the ones that were circulated from the beginning and deemed accurate portrayals of what took place, but that contradictory stories that have been known to surface came out at a much later date.

By focusing on these truths, we accomplish at least two things:

» 1) We realize our faith is rooted in historical events that did take place within history, and

» 2) We demonstrate to the critic that their arguments have no historical basis.

APPLICATION

Remind students of the "head to heart to hand" model found in Session 1, then direct them to spend time reflecting/writing on how this session challenges them both inwardly and outwardly.

PERSONAL:

1) How has the information in this session strengthened your personal faith in God?

MISSIONAL:

2) How has the information in this session help prepare you to answer the skeptics and share with the unsaved?

CONTINUE THE STORY

Direct students to review the story found at the beginning of this session. Ask them how they would respond to the brothers based upon what they have learned throughout this session?

SESSION 7

A LIKELY STORY

OPENING

Seat students in a circle. Explain to them that you are going to start a fictional story. You will not finish the story, but will stop at some point, then the person to your right will pick up the storyline and add to it. Then the person to their right will do the same, and continue this all around the circle until the story gets back to you. Point out that all of you have created quite a story.

> **» ASK:** Do you think our story is believable? Why or why not? What would you to do if you had to convince someone it was a true story?

Explain that your story is probably too far-fetched to be believable. Maybe as implausible as a story about a man rising from the dead.

THE STORY

While I certainly enjoy watching history shows on television, I usually avoid those that are talking about the Bible or Christianity in general. It's not that I don't learn from these, for I do – however, my learning is often only one sided since these shows tend to show only one perspective or overly biased reports. Nevertheless, one night I decided to not bypass the channel as I was flipping through the sea of entertainment options. The topic was the resurrection of Jesus. And at one point during the segment, one of the interviewers asked a bishop the following question: "what if you find out at the end of your life that Christianity isn't true? What if the resurrection never happened?" Without hesitation the bishop responds by saying, "I will have had no regrets since the Christian life is a fulfilling life."

After hearing the response, I thought to myself, "That's not what Paul would say." According to Paul, if the resurrection of Christ, which is foundational to the Christian life, did not take place, then Christians, of all people, are most to be pitied (1 Cor. 15: 12-19). Sure, the Christian life has a great value system and ethic in place to live by – but none of that matters if Christ has not been raised from the dead. Everything hinges on whether the resurrection took place or not. And Paul, someone bent on persecuting the church, bet everything, including his life, on the historicity of the resurrection based upon his personal encounter with the risen Lord on the road to Damascus.

» THE QUESTION

Call on a student to read the question for the session:
Did the resurrection actually happen?

FIRST RESPONSE

» **ASK:** If you had to answer that question today, how would you respond?

THE SKEPTIC'S VIEW

Discuss the skeptic's view of this issue using the information below.

As we draw our study to a close, it is helpful to explore the evidence we have for the historicity of the resurrection of Jesus. Like Paul, we want a reasoned faith—good grounds and evidences that support the things we believe. And having a reasoned faith and good grounds for believing in the truthfulness of the resurrection is central to a Christian's entire worldview. Why? Because if the resurrection did not happen, then Christianity is a sham. However, if it did happen, then everything in our lives will be effected by this single historical act. It is hugely significant for not only this life, but for life to come.

In order to see the evidence for the resurrection, let's first take a peak into the position of the skeptic. According to the skeptic, the resurrection of Jesus Christ simply did not take place. As far as trying to explain away the facts of Jesus' burial, the empty tomb, and the postresurrection appearances, the skeptic tries to offer other explanations to these events—explanations that, as you will see, are quite far-fetched.

So, when it comes to answering the skeptic and defending your beliefs in the resurrection, consider two ways of response: your personal experience of Christ and historical evidence. Since you probably have the first one down, let's look at the second one, the historical evidence, and let's see if the Christian's position is more intelligible than the skeptic's.

» THE RESPONSE

1) THE EVIDENCE THAT WON'T GO AWAY

There are three glaring historical evidences that the skeptic must deal with if they want to overturn the resurrection. These are:

1) The Burial Account
2) The Empty Tomb
3) The Post-resurrection Appearances

Surely there are other things the Christian can point to that only provides additional support in the resurrection, but this is a good working list. And the reason it is so good is because skeptics can't come up with a theory that adequately accounts for these facts.

Just take the second one as an example. Whatever theory makes the most sense to skeptics on any given day, their chosen model must at least involve the reality of an opened grave. Because when the story began circulating in the hours following Jesus' death, suggesting that He had been miraculously raised from the dead, one quick swing out to His final resting place would have been the only, simple, falling-off-a-log requirement to stop all this fanatical discussion. One body meant no story.

But obviously this wasn't the case.

> » **STATE AND DISCUSS:** "People can make whatever conjecture they please about the resurrection, from saying His body was probably stolen to wondering if it was ever actually placed there to begin with. But the tomb was empty. Somehow. By someone's hand. The fact that we're still talking about it today is ample proof of that."

- If nothing else seems to wash about the disciples' claim that Jesus came back to life after His crucifixion, the empty tomb at least remains a check in the asset column for them. It's consistent with their statement, whether you believe any of the rest of it or not.

On no reasonable grounds can anyone claim that Jesus' bones remained in Jesus' tomb, not by the third day after His death. The best we can tell, no one ever claimed to find Jesus' body or decayed remains. That would have ended all debate immediately. An empty tomb meant other options had to be raised. Fill-in-the-blank became the alternative.

» **ASK:** Why would the fact of the empty tomb prove to be difficult historical fact for the skeptic?

2) THE THEORIES

Use the following information to explain four different theories—three skeptical and one biblical—regarding the resurrection, pointing out which one is best able to account for all of the historical evidence. To help students with this section, icons of the historical evidences signify exactly what evidences each theory is able to explain, as well as which evidences they cannot account for. In the end, it will be shown that only the resurrection theory is best able to account for all three historical evidences.

THEORY #1: Hallucination THEORY

In an attempt to explain away the empty tomb and post-resurrection appearances, critics have argued that Jesus' disciples fell under a grief-induced trance and only imagined they saw Jesus alive—visibly present, speaking with them, grasping them around the shoulders, smiling, laughing, settling them down, cooking their breakfast. It's a lot for them to dream up, covering nearly a month and a half of face-to-face experiences, but that's the proposition as it stands—that he was only there in their mind's eye.

So his death, hard enough under any circumstances, was an unbearable blow to their lives and their futures. Mentally, spiritually, physically, emotionally. It's not hard to see, the skeptics say, how the disciples closest to Jesus could have become disoriented enough in mind—and desperate enough in their coping strategies—to perhaps conjure him up in a waking dream.

» **STATE AND DISCUSS:** Bottom Line: The disciples were just seeing things.

» **ASK:** How would you respond to the hallucination view?

Challenge the theory:

- How could eleven people (the number of remaining apostles after the suicide of Judas) all experience the same hallucination? Modern day experts say that would be impossible.[14]
- What about when five hundred people were on hand to see Jesus, all at the same time (1 Cor. 15:6)? Were the hallucinogens being passed around to every person in attendance? Was every one of his post-resurrection appearances conducted at some outdoor music festival?
- When Paul encountered the risen Christ on the road to Damascus, he certainly wasn't in a state of grief. He hated the very ground Jesus had walked on and wanted to destroy the movement. The vivid sight and sound of the risen Christ caught Paul completely out of the blue—the last thing he was possibly expecting. Where's the rationality in saying he was lost in a fog of altered emotions?
- And we still have an empty tomb, which had previously been sealed shut with a stone door and without a Jedi Master in sight. You don't just dream that into reality.

Therefore, the absence of Jesus' body works against the delirium hypothesis and in favor of the disciples' account. So, even though this theory is able to explain the burial account, it is unable to adaquately explain in a reasonable way the postresurrection appearances, nor does it at all account for the fact of the empty tomb.

THEORY #2: Conspiracy HYPOTHESIS

Another skeptical argument comes from what has traditionally been called the conspiracy hypothesis. The conspiracy views basically states that the disciples stole the body and lied about the resurrection. Their Jesus was dead, and they had some explaining to do. So by quickly going into tap-dancing mode, they went about creating a hoax they prayed would buy them enough time until they could figure out their next move—and then figure out how to keep selling it going forward. Making it up as they went along.

In fact, this view is not only sometimes still used today, but was first proposed by the Jewish authorities in the first century who attempted to silence the claim of the resurrection by working in collaboration with the Roman guards at the tomb. The view states that it was the disciples who were responsible for the empty tomb and the fabricated announcement of a resurrection.

» **STATE AND DISCUSS:** Bottom Line: The disciples stole His body and made the whole thing up.

» **ASK:** How would you respond to the conspiracy theory? Does it account for the evidences?

Challenge the theory:
- How can the conspiracy theory make sense of the post-resurrection appearances of Jesus to individuals like Paul and James, as well as many others who were not close followers and/or disciples? According to Paul, there were over 500 eye-witness reports of Jesus' post-resurrection appearances. How can it explain these facts? It simply can't.
- The theory itself fails to adequately account for the historic evidence of the disciples fleeing the scene as a result of cowardice, going into hiding, and/or returning to their homes and former professions.
- Nor does it take into consideration, as William Lane Craig says, "the disciples' evident sincerity and willingness to be martyred for their faith." People can run on steam for only a little while. If it was a lie, eventually the weight of maintaining their story would have brought down the charade. A lie, after all, is a terrible thing to live for. It's an even harder thing to die for.

Read and discuss the following quote:
"What's interesting about the disciples is that no one ever cut a deal. Not once, while facing torture, crucifixion or imprisonment, did a disciple turn on the others. No last-minute confessions or public declarations denouncing the resurrection hoax."[15]

- The usual pattern when concocting a piece of hasty fiction is to build a watertight case by adding layers of detail you would expect your audience to believe and accept. If that's the case, then why leave themselves out of the starring roles. Instead, they did something no first-century Jew would have done, they made women a prominent part of their story. Women weren't even permitted to testify in a court of law at this period in history, except in specific cases like sexual abuse. [16] They would hardly have made the most believable eyewitnesses and first responders to the risen Christ to be women if the story was made up.Thus, even though this theory agrees with the burial account and tries to explain the empty tomb, its version of why the tomb is empty does not stand up to the other evidence we have. Moreover, the theory is completely unable to explain the postresurrection appearances.

▸ When it comes down to it, you've got an unlikely story, an unimpressed audience, risks of an untimely death, and a totally uncommon cast of characters. The claim that the disciples fabricated a culturally unpopular idea (resurrection), used people who do not count as witnesses for it (women), presented it to a host of unbelieving followers (doubting disciples) as the way to persuade a doubting audience, is a gullible theory to buy.

THEORY #3: Mistaken Death THEORY

A third skeptical option that has been suggested is one that has traditionally been called the apparent death theory. According to this view, Jesus was not in fact dead when taken off the cross – he only appeared to have been. It was only later, after laying in the coolness of the tomb, that Jesus was able to be revived and have his energy restored.

» **STATE AND DISCUSS:** Bottom Line: Jesus never completely died.

» **ASK:** What do you think about this theory? How would you respond against it?

Challenge the theory:
- The medical background knowledge that we now have, in conjunction with the historic details of Roman crucifixion practices, makes the hypothesis highly suspect.
- The details of the historic account confirm the fact that the Roman practitioners of the crucifixion made sure of Jesus' death by piercing His side as opposed to breaking His legs.

Once again, this skeptical explanation falls short of providing a coherent and compelling explanation of all the known facts. Even though their theory attempts to explain the main three key pieces of evidence, it utterly fails in that attempt in light of the other known evidences we have. When you begin to postulate random and borderline absurd theories as potential explanations, you move from the evidence to simple wishful thinking.

THEORY #4: THE Resurrection THEORY

The final theory to consider is the one made by eyewitnesses and Christians during the first century – that God raised Jesus from the dead. Where all other theories fail to adequately explain the evidence, the resurrection theory sufficiently explains all of the details that must be addressed, such as:

- the burial account
- the empty tomb
- the post resurrection appearances
- the conversion of Paul and James
- the disciples' willingness to face persecution and death

There are additional reasons we could mention that demonstrate the resurrection theory to be a better explanation of the data than any other theory—but these will have to do for now. Therefore, based upon this evidence, it would be unreasonable for one to not seriously consider the resurrection theory to be the best explanation of the evidence. It explains, without far-fetched ideas, the evidences that we know – the burial account, the empty tomb, and the postresurrection appearances. This just goes to show that if one rejected the resurrection theory, it wouldn't be because the evidence led them to reject it. There would have to be some non-evidential reasons.

» **STATE AND DISCUSS:** Bottom Line: Jesus really did rise from the dead.

» **ASK:** Why is it important to emphasize that all of the evidence points to the truth of the resurrection?

GROUP DISCUSSION

» 1) What are some of the alternative explanations for the empty tomb and claims made by eyewitnesses that Jesus rose from the dead? What are some of the problems with these alternative explanations?

» 2) What do you think is the biggest evidence in support of the resurrection? Explain.

» 3) What is significant about women being the first eyewitnesses to the resurrection?

» 4) Why is it important to note that the skeptics' arguments are all naturalistic? How does this limit their perspective? What evidence do they have to support a naturalistic understanding?

» 5) Why should even skeptics want the resurrection to be true?

CLOSING THOUGHTS

Discuss the closing thoughts to help summarize and reinforce the main points of this session.

All of the arguments against the resurrection have something in common—they are all naturalistic. What does that mean? Well, it means that the explanations themselves will never look for a supernatural explanation, only natural. Even if the evidences point to a supernatural explanation, the naturalist will not allow himself to entertain that possibility. By doing so, he limits and confines himself, not allowing the evidence to lead where it will.

If our opponents arguments fail to stand up to the evidence, and if our arguments are the most reasonable and offer a better explanation of the evidence we do have, then it follows that the resurrection was one of the central messages of the New Testament. Central because it was historical—it actually happened. But also because of what it meant for both life now and life to come.

The fact of the empty tomb is still today the most powerful argument to silence the critic. It not only allows one to see how her or her rival view fails, but also puts one in a position to answer for himself who he believes Jesus Christ to be. There is no walking away from this question or taking a pass on answering. It is a question of utter importance, affecting both life here and life to come. Thankfully, for the Christian, there are solid reasons in affirming the truth that Jesus is Lord and that He rose from the dead.

By focusing on these truths, we accomplish at least two things:

» 1) We gain a better assurance that our faith is historically reliable.

» 2) We show the skeptic that all of his arguments against the resurrection fail as an adequate alternative.

APPLICATION

Remind students of the "head to heart to hand" model found in Session 1, then direct them to spend time reflecting/writing on how this session challenges them both inwardly and outwardly.

PERSONAL:

1) How has the information in this session strengthened your personal faith in God?

MISSIONAL:

2) How has the information in this session help prepare you to answer the skeptics and share with the unsaved?

» CONTINUE THE STORY

Direct students to review the story found at the beginning of this session. Ask them how they would respond to a friend who struggles to believe in the validity of the resurrection, based upon what they have learned throughout this session?

Take a moment to review the whole study with your students.

- » **ASK:** Which of the seven questions do you believe is the most prevelent among your friends? Do you feel better equipped to discuss this with them? Why or why not?

- » **ASK:** How has this study helped you prepare to defend your faith? Which of the seven questions do you feel least equipped to discuss? Why?

Encourge students that the apologetics conversation needs to continue. Take note of the questions they felt weakest to answer and perhaps schedule another time to discuss those and other questions they raise.

NOTES

SESSION 2

1. Keller, *The Reason for God: Belief in an Age of Skepticism* (New York: Penguin, 2008), 74-75.
2. Alvin Plantinga, "A Christian Life Partly Lived," in *Philosphers Who Believe: The Spiritual Journeys of 11 Leading Thinkers*, ed. Kelly James Clark (Downers Grove: Intervarsity, 1997), 72.

SESSION 3

3. Haer, 3.11.8.
4. See Bruce M. Metzger, *The Canon of the New Testament* (Oxford: Clarendon, 1987), 305–7.

SESSION 5

5. Bruce M. Metzger and Bart D. Ehrman, *The Text of the New Testament: Its Transmission, Corruption, and Restoration*, 4th ed. (New York: Oxford University Press, 2005), 86.
6. For a succinct introduction to textual criticism, see Bruce M. Metzger, *A Textual Commentary on the Greek New Testament*, 2d. ed. (New York: UBS, 1994), 1–16.

SESSION 6

7. The only first-century evidence for controversy reveals some Jewish groups who embraced Jesus but questioned his deity (the Ebionites).
8. The classic treatment on Gnosticism is Edwin Yamauchi, *Pre-Christian Gnosticism: A Survey of the Proposed Evidences* (Grand Rapids: Eerdmans, 1973).
9. See Kostenberger and Kruger, Heresy of Orthodoxy, chapter 3, esp. 89-98.
10. For a survey of the major sects of the second century, see Antti Marjanen and Petri Luomanen, eds., *A Companion to Second-Century Christian "Heretics,"* Supplements to Vigiliae Christianae 76 (Leiden: Brill, 2005).
11. Paul embarked on at least three missionary journeys, commonly dated to the years 47-48, 49-51, and 51-54. See, e.g., Andreas J. Kostenberger, L. Scott Kellum, and Charles L. Quarles, *Cradle, the Cross, and the Brown: An Introduction to the New Testament* (Nashville: B&H Academic, 2009), 391-94.
12. See the concluding chapter in Bock's *The Missing Gospels*, where a survey of these writings shows that almost all of them mention in one way or another what this core theology was.
13. Kostenberger and Kruger, *Heresy of Orthodoxy*, 66.

SESSION 7

14. James Porter Moreland. *Scaling the Secular City: a Defense of Christianity.* (Grand Rapids, MI: Baker Book House, 1987.) 177.
15. Moreland, *The God Conversation*, 87-88.
16. Richard Bauckham, *Gospel Women: Studies of the Named Women in the Gospels* (Grand Rapids: Eerdmans/Edinburgh: T&T Clark, 2002), 268–77; cf. N. T. Wright, Resurrection of the Son of God (Christian Origins and the Question of God, vol. 3) (Minneapolis: Fortress, 2003), 607. See also ancient Jewish texts such as m. Shebuot 4.1; Rosh Hashanah 1.8; b. Baba Qamma 88a that show how consistent this idea was across the centuries of Jewish tradition, even after the time of Jesus.

NOTES